The 3-Week Miracle

A Step-by-Step Guide to a More Successful Life

DR. KRIS HEAP

ISBN: 0983682402
ISBN-13: 9780983682400

This book is dedicated to:

My amazing wife, Sarah,
for putting up with an eccentric dreamer.

To my parents, who taught me that serving others
is the greatest work we can do.

And to the
Young Men and Women of the Boulder Mountain Ward.
Who prove that our future is even brighter
than our past.
You are a miracle!

PREFACE

Let's start a movement. Not a movement backed by big money or some large special-interest group. Not a movement to gain any kind of rights or freedoms.

Let's start a movement for ourselves. We deserve it, right? We spend a lot of time helping others, working for others and admiring others. What about us?

Let's start a movement full of people who are dedicated to bettering our families, our communities, and our world. Not in the way that most people would think. Our movement is all about us, without being selfish or self-centered.

Our movement is made up of individuals who are reclaiming their hopes and dreams of a better, more fulfilling life. Those dreams that were put aside because of work, or children, or laziness. Those dreams that we are sometimes afraid to dream or to talk about out loud. The dreams we hold deep inside.

Our movement is made up entirely of people who want to be better, do more, and live life more fully. We are the people who know that change requires effort; and we are ready to put forth the effort.

Our movement will teach others that happiness and success can be had by all. It will call to those who are discouraged, depressed, and disillusioned. It will call to the housewife and the business owner. It will call to the student and the teacher. It will call to the poor and the wealthy.

Our movement will improve the world, because it will improve the people in the world. Not through one great, explosive event; but through small and simple successes magnified by the thousands of people joining our ranks.

It is time. Time to do more. Time to be more. Time to show the world that we are not common, we are not average, we are not going to passively become what the world wants us to become. We are meant for more. We are ready to learn and put forth the effort required for success.

It starts with us. It starts today.
This is <u>our</u> movement.
Turn the page and let's get started.

- Kris Heap
www.3WeekMiracle.com

The 3-Week Miracle

INTRODUCTION

On a hot August evening in Mesa, Arizona, a player wearing jersey #24 runs onto the football field. He is the starting middle linebacker for the Mesa Community College Thunderbirds. Underneath the pads and uniform, however, there is something different about this player; something that the crowd in the stands doesn't realize. #24 is about to live his lifelong dream.

Lincoln Proctor is from St. John's, Arizona, a small town near the New Mexico border. He played football in high school and then left the country to serve a 2-year mission for his church in Ecuador.

Upon his return, he worked for a company building custom iron fences. In 2006, he started a business in the iron fence industry. As the economy turned, so did the business and he eventually closed up shop. He spent some time in different jobs and eventually decided to go back to school. He enrolled at Mesa Community College. Soon after enrolling, he found out there would be open try-outs for the football team. He got excited. When he was young he had dreamed of playing college football. The he remembered something; he was 32 years old! He has a young family at home. There is no way a 32-year old man could go out and compete with young athletes in their prime. Or could he? Lincoln decided to take chance at living his dream.

It wasn't easy. He was competing with 80 other kids for just a few open spots on the team. "What the heck am I doing?" he asked himself. Many of the other players were stronger and faster but he was determined to make up for it in hard work and maximum effort. He would show the coaches that he wanted this more than anybody else.

Thirty minutes before the try-out started he realized that he needed a physical release from a doctor to be able to play. In a panic, he ran across the street to an urgent care who just happened to offer physicals. There was a long line, so he went around asking if anyone would trade numbers with him. When he was finally able to see the doctor, they wouldn't sign his physical because the running and anxiety had pushed his blood pressure through the roof. After some tense moments, his blood pressure came down. He got his physical release, ran back across the street, and played his heart out. When try-outs were over, the coach pulled him aside and told him he had made the team.

Lincoln wasn't done yet. With hard work and desire he earned the starting role as middle linebacker. He kept working. The program awarded him a football scholarship. He kept working. The coaches named him as a defensive captain. Lincoln is 12 years older than the average player on the team. His nicknames among the players are "Grandpa" or "Father Time". He is still working.

On August 13th, 2011, while the crowd came to watch the Thunderbirds play, a small group was cheering wildly for a man who was living his dream.

When you ask him how it is going, a smile crosses his lips as he says, "I'm having the time of my life! It should be illegal to have this much fun!"

Is Lincoln Proctor super-human? No. Is he more capable than everyone else? No. He is a man who had a dream. Even when conventional wisdom would say that his window of opportunity had closed, he took a chance. He got out on the field and put in the effort. It is hard and painful work but he is having the time of his life. He's not done. He's hoping to transfer and play for a major university. He is living the dream.

Lincoln is part of a new movement of people who are fed up with living life on auto-pilot. The people in this movement are not the incredibly talented or ambitious. They are your friends, neighbors, co-workers, and family members. They are the average, everyday people around you. There is one difference though. They are starting to realize that they are not average. They are rediscovering the dreams they once had. They are learning that working towards their true dreams will bring them happiness, confidence and fulfillment. They are experiencing the miracle.

How about you?

If someone asked you to describe your life, what would you say? Is it the way you always hoped it would be? Are you on track to accomplish your goals and dreams? Do you have goals? Could you even list or describe them if you had to?

How about your relationships? Are they strong and mutually fulfilling? Are you getting as much out of them as you are putting in?

How confident are you in yourself? Do you like who you are? Do you hide who you are? Do you feel that you have something to offer everyone around you?

Are you happy? Do you find your work fulfilling? Do you have a "bucket list" of experiences you're dreaming about completing? Do you feel you will ever really do them?

I hope you could answer positively to all of these questions. But I know that if you are anything like me (or if you're human at all), there are a lot of things you would like to improve. It's okay. Everybody does.

What if you could change your life in just 21 days?

What if I said that in 3 weeks you could alter the course of your entire future for the better? What if I said it would only take you about 30 minutes per day? It would be worth it, right? Of course it would! You can make it happen. It isn't magic. It will take hard work and dedication on your part but, in the end, it will feel like a miracle. Like you've unlocked some kind of great secret of success.

The real secret of life is this: You hold the power. You always have. You already have everything you need to accomplish whatever you want. It doesn't matter if your goal is making more money, losing more weight, being happy, dropping an addiction, having less stress or just having a defined vision of where your life is going. You already have everything you need right inside of you. You just have to find a way to let it out!

There are hundreds of self-help books out there that give different insights into unlocking your potential and experiencing true happiness. This book is a little bit different. There is some work involved. It is designed to be a workbook that will teach you the basic principles of success, help you to internalize them, and then make them a part of your daily life. Amazingly, it doesn't take as long as you might think to see major results. All you need to get started is a desire to change. From there, it only takes a little effort each day to achieve greatness. If you have the desire, you can do it.

Will it work for you? It will if you let it. You bought the book so you have already expressed a desire to improve your life. Whether it is a small desire or even just curiosity, it can be enough to start the chain reaction that will lead to major change.

This book was developed as I studied the principles and habits of the people I admired most in many areas of life. I collected stories and biographies of people that inspired me. The more I studied these people, the more I began to realize something important. I realized that there are definite, repeatable actions and skills that all of these people have developed that make them great. Not only that, these skills could be learned and mastered by anybody who was willing to put forth the effort! What an exciting discovery! People aren't born naturally great and successful. Success can be learned. It can be developed. It can be mastered. If others have done it, you can do it.

That's the main idea I hope you get from reading this book:

The secrets of becoming successful, no matter how you define success, have nothing to do with external factors but everything to do with a person's inner

commitment to be great. All men and women are endowed with greatness and designed to succeed. Greatness can be taught, it can be learned, and it can be achieved by anyone.

That's it. Plain and simple. Becoming successful in life is not some magical power that some are born with and others are left without. It is not some secret, hidden away for only a few to discover. It comes from a personal commitment, some faith in oneself, and the repetition of a few powerful principles that I will share in this book. All men and women of great success and stature have utilized some, if not all, of these principles in their life. So can you. These habits will not only allow you to achieve your goals, but you can do it faster than you ever thought possible.

How do I know it works? I have tested it and seen it work in my own life. When I started to incorporate what I found, I noticed amazing results in all aspects of my life. I became happier, healthier, more grateful, more positive, more efficient with my time, and more successful. I was amazed at how much I was able to accomplish in a short time. It was like my life was accelerating toward my long-term goals.

I definitely wasn't born doing these things. I didn't spend very much of my life doing these things. I've had to force myself to learn and apply these principles. It did not come naturally. But it has become easier and easier.

Being the person you want to be is a conscious effort that anyone can accomplish. Decide to do it, put in the effort, and become what you have always dreamed of becoming.

Some People Aren't Ready for This Book

There are some people who aren't ready for this book. It will only have its full effect on the person who is truly ready to: 1) accept responsibility for their past, 2) put in the effort to change their present and, 3) work towards a clearly defined future.

It is not for the person who says, "Hey, I like money and I want a quick way to get more of it." You will not be instantly rich because you read this book for three weeks. You will, however, be more successful if you apply the principles. You may end up making a lot more money because of it. But it is by no means a quick fix. It will take commitment, dedication, and hard work.

It is not for the person who cannot accept responsibility for their past choices. We are all in our current situation solely because of our own life decisions. If you think that you lack happiness because of some hard circumstance or the actions of someone else, you are wrong. You don't always decide what happens to you, but you decide how you will react to it. You make your life decisions. You have to own them. You decide how you feel inside, nobody else. You decide how you will act from day to day, nobody else. Where you are now in life is the sum of all the decisions you have made up to this point.

This book is not for the casual reader. This book is designed as a workbook, with a heavy emphasis on the word "work". There are a lot of great "feel-good" stories and anecdotes contained in this book but they are all designed to teach a principle and then push you into action. This book will be exciting for the person who is prepared to improve their life. It will seem like a waste of time to the person who is not ready.

Who Is Ready for This Book?

This book is for the person who has sincerely looked at their life and found areas where they would like to improve. Some will use this book to become more successful in business. Some will use it to become happier or add greater spirituality to their daily life. Others will use this to rid themselves of destructive habits, replacing them with positive actions. Some will love it; some will think it is a waste of time. This book will be completely different for each reader. It is completely adaptable to any situation. Why? Because the principles of success are the same anywhere they are applied. This book can help any reader to:

- Improve their general happiness
- Have a positive attitude all of the time
- Develop an attitude of gratitude
- Become less offended by the actions of others
- Increase spirituality
- Have stronger family relationships
- Raise emotionally stable and successful children
- Succeed in business
- Leave behind destructive habits
- Recover from substance abuse
- Gain confidence
- Have more friends

- Become healthier or lose weight
- Increase their earning potential
- Obtain their life goals faster than they ever thought possible

When I type it all out, it sounds like a magic bullet type of solution doesn't it? Well, it is! Major corporations pay consultants millions of dollars to teach these same principles to their executives. These principles are used in Alcoholics Anonymous to help addicts overcome substance abuse. They are taught by the greatest psychologists and family counselors in the world. They are practiced by the most successful people in any industry. From executives to Olympians to Nobel Prize Winners, the principles work for them, and they will work for you. You just have to be willing to put in the effort to learn them and commit them into your daily habits. So let's get going!

Making It Work for You

In this book we will talk about the natural laws of success in an organized way, letting one build on another. Each day you will have the opportunity to read about one of these laws and develop a plan to incorporate it into your daily life.

The book is called *The Three-Week Miracle* because it is based on the idea that it takes 21 days of repetitive action to form a habit. Or, said in a different way, it takes three weeks of doing something every day for it to sink into our subconscious and become a part of us. Three weeks is not much to ask. It is achievable. If we can form good habits and put positive thoughts into our head for three weeks, we will see an amazing change in how we feel and what we can accomplish.

The goal, however, is not to develop habits that just last us through the 21 days, but that we develop the habits that will last us through the rest of our lives. This book is intended to be the spark that starts the fire.

Here's how it works:

Today you will read the introduction, take a brief quiz and answer a few questions. This will give you your starting point.

Tomorrow you will start with "Day 1", which will help you develop the vision for your life. Be prepared to spend about 30-45 minutes for "Day 1". It is the most important step and is the only one that will take you longer than about 15 minutes.

Each day after that will have a new principle to learn. Read the paragraphs about the highlighted principle and then proceed with the writing activity associated for that day. **Do this <u>every</u> morning before your day gets going.** The longer you wait into the day, the harder it becomes to get it done.

It is important that you stick to <u>one principle per day</u>. The principles build upon one another. You can always go back and reread pages you have completed. But if you start reading ahead, you will most likely start skipping the writing assignments and therefore deprive yourself of the benefits of the program. The power of this book comes from the daily repetition of powerful ideas. Don't cheat yourself out of their effectiveness.

At the end of the day you will have the opportunity to reflect on your day and write about what you experienced. This will help to engrain the ideas in your mind but also allow you to review your areas of success and your opportunities for improvement. This is a wonderful time to write about how you are feeling with the progress you are making or the areas you are struggling with. <u>It is best to do this just before going to bed.</u>

If you miss a day, just keep going as though you hadn't missed. Some people have difficulty staying with the program on the weekends. If that happens, just start back up on Monday. If you miss multiple days, you may want to go back a few pages and review before proceeding. The lessons can be learned individually but I hope you have made the commitment to dedicate yourself to this program for 21 straight days. To get the results you want, you need to put in the effort to deserve them.

Let's Get Started!

Well, you are ready to go! A few words of advice before you start:

- Make a deep, inner commitment to attack this program with all of your energy. Your results are directly related to the effort you put in, so please don't settle for a partial effort.
- Leave your past behind you. Today is a new day and you will be a new person. Ralph Waldo Emerson once said, *"What lies behind us and what lies before us are tiny matters compared to what lies within us."* Dare to push yourself to be more. Don't let your past hold you back. It is past. Move on.

- Give it time. My experience has been that you will notice big results within the first few days. But if you don't see immediate results, don't be discouraged. You will. It is impossible to go through these practices without affecting your thoughts and actions for the better.

- The best way to make sure you do this every day is to have a trigger; something you do every day that will remind you to read the book. For example, hopefully you shower every day. Decide that you will read every day before taking a shower. That should make sure you do it. I do mine right when I get to work before seeing my first patient. The reading and writing only take about 10-15 minutes so it shouldn't be hard to find a small time first thing in the morning to do it.

- You will get out of it what you put into it. If you do it every day it will work. If you don't, it probably won't. It's up to you.

"Whatever you can conceive and believe, you can achieve!"

- Napoleon Hill

My Commitment to Myself

I, _____ , commit myself to achieving personal success. I will make this program a daily priority.

I recognize that I am not currently all that I want to be and therefore I am willing to spend time every day developing the habits that will lead to happiness, success and the realization of my goals.

I will leave behind all feelings of doubt, low self-esteem, skepticism and negativity. I will not get discouraged or frustrated with myself as I work through this program. I deserve great things in life and I am capable of achieving them.

As I follow this program, I will take action every day to set my goals and to work towards their completion. I am willing to put temporary pleasures aside in order to focus on my long-term happiness.

I understand that I will get out of this program what I put into it. I will work hard to complete each activity so that I may see the results I desire.

I will not give up on myself. I will see this through to the end.
Today I take control of my future.

_____

Signature   Date

Initial Assessment

"Know Thyself"

I believe that for us to start the endeavor of self-improvement we need to first know where we are starting. This is called self-awareness. As you grow in self-awareness, you will better understand why you feel what you feel and why you behave as you behave. That understanding then gives you the opportunity and freedom to change those things you'd like to change about yourself and create the life you want. Without fully knowing who you are, self-acceptance and change become impossible.

On the following page is a self-assessment questionnaire that is designed to help you reflect on where you see yourself in a number of areas. The most important requirement of this questionnaire is that you be honest with yourself. If you truly feel you score well in an area, score yourself high. If you feel you need to improve, score yourself lower. This exercise is not intended to make you feel down if you have an overall low score. It is merely to take a snapshot of where you are on Day 1. You will take a similar quiz at the end of the 21 days so you can see what progress you have made.

Please complete all questions. Rate each answer on a scale of 1-5. Select the answer that best represents your feelings, thoughts, and behaviors as they relate to your current situation. Remember to answer as openly and honestly as possible. You are the only one who will see the results.

Turn to the next page and choose how true each statement is for you.

STATEMENT	ASSESSMENT	SCORE
HOPE		
I believe in my ability to change my life.	Less True 1 2 3 4 5 More True	
I see my financial situation improving in the next 5 years.	Less True 1 2 3 4 5 More True	
I believe that I can be happy.	Less True 1 2 3 4 5 More True	
I feel optimistic about the future.	Less True 1 2 3 4 5 More True	
I face adversity and opposition calmly and with hope.	Less True 1 2 3 4 5 More True	
	Total Score for Section =	
	Average Score (Total/5) =	

STATEMENT	ASSESSMENT	SCORE
PERSONAL MANAGEMENT		
I put time into improving my job skills.	Less True 1 2 3 4 5 More True	
I put time into improving myself.	Less True 1 2 3 4 5 More True	
I know the principles to employ that will make me successful.	Less True 1 2 3 4 5 More True	
I am efficient with my time.	Less True 1 2 3 4 5 More True	
I tend to my responsibilities without being asked.	Less True 1 2 3 4 5 More True	
I am willing to work hard to improve myself.	Less True 1 2 3 4 5 More True	
I focus my thoughts on positive ideas and goals.	Less True 1 2 3 4 5 More True	
I do something to better myself every day.	Less True 1 2 3 4 5 More True	
I gratefully accept advice, correction and criticism.	Less True 1 2 3 4 5 More True	
I work hard, even when I'm not under pressure or close supervision.	Less True 1 2 3 4 5 More True	

I focus my efforts on the most important things.	Less True 1 2 3 4 5 More True	
I keep a balance between work, family, rest and self-improvement.	Less True 1 2 3 4 5 More True	
I am patient with myself as I overcome challenges and obstacles.	Less True 1 2 3 4 5 More True	
I am always punctual.	Less True 1 2 3 4 5 More True	
	Total Score for Section	
	Average Score (Total/14) =	

Personal Worth and Self-Esteem		
I believe in my ability to become successful.	Less True 1 2 3 4 5 More True	
I feel confident in who I am and the choices I make.	Less True 1 2 3 4 5 More True	
I am grateful for that which I have.	Less True 1 2 3 4 5 More True	
I am happy with the amount of money I make.	Less True 1 2 3 4 5 More True	
I enjoy my current job.	Less True 1 2 3 4 5 More True	
I feel I have something positive to offer those around me.	Less True 1 2 3 4 5 More True	
I am genuinely happy when others around me succeed.	Less True 1 2 3 4 5 More True	
	Total Score for Section	
	Average Score (Total/7) =	

Goals and Vision		
I have a clearly defined vision of where I want to be in 5 years.	Less True 1 2 3 4 5 More True	
I have clearly-written long and short-term goals.	Less True 1 2 3 4 5 More True	
I set daily goals for myself	Less True 1 2 3 4 5 More True	
I review my actions from the day and look for ways to improve them.	Less True 1 2 3 4 5 More True	
	Total Score for Section	
	Average Score (Total/4) =	

Love and Charity		
I show gratitude to the people who help and support me.	Less True 1 2 3 4 5 More True	
I make time to be with my family and loved ones.	Less True 1 2 3 4 5 More True	
I enjoy the benefits of a strong family.	Less True 1 2 3 4 5 More True	
I forgive those who have offended or wronged me.	Less True 1 2 3 4 5 More True	
I treat my family with love and respect all of the time.	Less True 1 2 3 4 5 More True	
I actively look for ways to help other people.	Less True 1 2 3 4 5 More True	
I try to understand the feelings of others and their point of view.	Less True 1 2 3 4 5 More True	
	Total Score for Section	
	Average Score (Total/7) =	

Total Test Score	
(Add Total Scores from each section)	
Total / 37 = Average Score	

Now that you have completed the assessment, take a moment to look back over your responses and reflect on those where you scored yourself the lowest. Those 4-5 questions where you scored the lowest are your "**Limiting Factors**". Put a small dash or star next to them. You've heard the saying that a chain is only as strong as its weakest link. Your Limiting Factors are the weakest links that are keeping you from progressing. For some it will be in the areas of hope or self-esteem. Others have difficulty showing gratitude. Many have a hard time with efficiency and time-management. Whatever yours are, know that for as good as you become in all other areas, you are only as strong as your weakest links.

Directly opposed to your Limiting Factors will be your "**Strengths**". These are the areas where you scored yourself the highest. Put a little plus sign next to these. Some of these come naturally to you and some of them you have worked hard to develop. Many of them you developed as a child without even realizing it by the way your parents raised you. These are the attributes that draw others to you and have been the source of the good works you have done.

Your goal should be to turn your "Limiting Factors" into "Strengths". Hellen Keller once said, "I thank God for my handicaps, for through them, I have found myself, my work and my God." As you progress through this book you will set goals and daily action plans for yourself. Many of these goals will deal directly with improving on your Limiting Factors. Every "Limiting Factor" can become a "Strength" with a little work.

You were not born being always late. You were not born with low self-esteem. You were not born to be unhappy with your life. These are behaviors that we have learned and developed over time. Because you learned them, you can unlearn them. And from there you can improve upon them and decide to be more and do better.

Remember, you were born for greatness and designed to succeed. Where you are now is merely the launch pad. Decide today that you will be better tomorrow.

Self-Assessment Worksheet

"I myself am made entirely of flaws, stitched together with good intentions."

- Augusten Burroughs

Challenge: Review the results of your self-assessment and look at the areas where you scored the highest and lowest. Identify the 3 attributes that you passionately want to convert from "Limiting Factors" into "Strengths" in the next 3 weeks.

What 2 areas had the highest averages? (Strengths)

1. _____

2. _____

What 5 questions received my lowest scores? (Limiting Factors)

1. _____

2. _____

3. _____

4. _____

5. _____

Which areas do I most strongly want to improve?

1. _____

2. _____

3. _____

STOP!

You've done a great job making it this far.
You have taken the first steps in this exciting process.
Tomorrow you will start the 3-week miracle!

Today you are the product of your past.

Tomorrow you will create your future.

WEEK 1

The Laws

DAY 1

DATE: _____

THE LAW OF VISION

"I can teach anybody how to get what they want out of life. The problem is that I can't find anybody who can tell me what they want."
— Mark Twain

A Chinese proverb says, "The journey of a thousand leagues begins with a single step." This chapter represents that single step. It is the beginning of your journey towards happiness, confidence and success.

As with any journey, you have to know where you are going if you plan to get anywhere. If you don't know where you are going, guess what...you are already there! It isn't where you want to be. It's just where you've been stuck.

It is safe to assume that if you made it through the introduction and have started on Day 1, you have the desire to move on from where you currently are. But to where? That is up to you. For your Day 1 exercise you are going to decide your destination. And I'll show you how. Get a pen ready.

A View from the Summit

The first thing you are going to do is take a second to sit back comfortably in your chair, take a few deep breaths and relax.

Now I want you to imagine that you were given a magic wand. You can wave that wand and make your life absolutely perfect. You can have everything you ever wanted and you can't fail at anything you try to do. What would that perfect life look like? Describe it. Don't worry how outrageous some of the ideas are. It's your ideal future. Nobody is looking so don't be embarrassed. Don't hold back because you think you can't obtain it or don't deserve to have it. Just pretend that you can have it all. Be as detailed as possible. Include all areas of your life including any areas from the self-assessment you want to improve upon.

- What goals would you like to accomplish?
- What would you do for work?
- What is your income?
- Where would you like to travel?
- How are your relationships with your friends, family, work associates?
- Where would you live?
- What would you do for fun?
- What hobbies do you have?

Now, on the next page, write down everything you saw and imagined in as much detail as possible. The more details you add, the more your brain will begin writing it into your subconscious. I'm going to push you to fill in at least 10 key components of your ideal life. The first 5 will probably come easily; the second 5 will require some effort. Whatever you write, make sure it is what you really want for your future. Don't hold back. Dare to dream!

Remember to be as specific as possible. **Always make sure to write them in the present tense as though you have already achieved them**. Examples: "I make.... per year.", "I live in.....", "I travel to ..... on vacation every year.", "I read 1 book per week.", etc. It may help to ask yourself, "If I were at the end of my life, I would feel incredibly sad if I never accomplished _____.

My Vision Statement

1.

2.

3.

4.

5.

6.

7.

8.

9.

10.

Now that you have envisioned your ideal life, you know where you want to go. That is exciting! You've probably never really thought about your ideal life in such detail and I'm almost positive you have never written it down. Less than .1% of people ever have. You are now in an elite group of those who have a clearly defined destination for their life. Congratulations!

This is your personal vision of your future. This vision will focus your goals and actions. Every decision you make will have to stack up against the vision you have developed. To every decision you will ask, "Does this choice get me closer to my vision?" If it doesn't, then why do it? Why would you want to? Why take a step that leads you away from your definite purpose in life?

This is called summit thinking. You've just imagined yourself at the summit of an enormous mountain of accomplishment. From the top you can look down and see the path that led you to the top as it winds it's way through deep crevasses and over steep climbs. You are starting this process from the end as though you have already attained everything you ever wanted.

Now it's just a matter of working backwards and filling in those points along the path. Those points are your short-term goals. And when you have strung together a series of successful, short-term goals, you will have reached that summit.

"You've got to think about big things while you're doing small things, so that all the small things go in the right direction."
— Alvin Toffler

With your vision in place and written down, you are ready to take the steps in the right direction. You are prepared to learn the principles that will aid you in your journey and accelerate the pace of attainment. In the next section you will learn how to develop the steps that will move you closer to your ideal life.

You know what you want, let's work on getting it.

"Destiny is not a matter of chance, but of choice.
Not something to wish for, but to attain."
— William Jennings Bryan

Vision Statement Notes

Use this space to reflect on the items you wrote down in your vision statement. Anything that you were surprised to find that didn't make the list? Anything that really excites you? How would it feel to have accomplished even one of these goals?

_____

_____

_____

_____

_____

_____

_____

_____

_____

_____

_____

_____

_____

_____

_____

_____

_____

DAY 1 WORKSHEET

THE VISION

"The greatest danger for most of us is not that our aim is too high and we miss it, but that it is too low and we reach it."

- Michaelangelo

Challenge: Look back at the 10 aspects of your ideal future and write down the 5 items you are the most passionate about accomplishing.

List the five items on your vision list that you are the <u>most</u> passionate about achieving:

1. _____

2. _____

3. _____

4. _____

5. _____

Which two do you feel will be the hardest to accomplish?

1. _____

_____

2. _____

_____

What do you feel will be the biggest obstacle in achieving your vision?

_____

_____

_____

What can you do today to take a step towards your vision?

_____

_____

_____

Additional Notes

_____

_____

_____

_____

_____

_____

_____

_____

_____

_____

_____

_____

DAY 2

DATE: _____

THE LAW OF DEFINITE PURPOSE

Now that you have a vision of where your life will be in the next 5-10 years, we need to develop the stepping-stones that will get you there. If you feel truly passionate and sincere about your vision for the future, the steps leading up to it will become your "**definite purpose**". It has also been called a "flight plan". Your definite purpose is your main focus. It is the most important work you will do this year because it will lead to your ideal future. Your definite purpose is made up of short-term, personal goals. Today we will do two exercises to help build your definite purpose.

The first exercise is to re-read your vision from yesterday and, keeping that in mind, pick 10 goals you would like to achieve <u>this year</u>. Some of them may be word for word from your Vision Statement, if you feel you could achieve them this year. Most of them will be intermediate steps that get you part way to your vision.

For example, if your ideal future vision is to make $400,000 per year, your goal for this year may say: "I have found 1 additional source of income" or "I have asked my boss for a 10% raise" or maybe "I have returned to school to get my degree."

If one of your Vision Statement items is, "I travel around the world to exotic places" you may make a goal this year to travel to a neighboring state you have never visited or even to a part of Canada or Mexico.

Maybe in your Vision Statement it says, "I show gratitude to all those around me." Your goal this year could be: "Every day I tell one person how much I appreciate them."

My own Vision Statement says, "I write books that help people improve their lives and I am paid to lecture around the world." My goal for this year was, "I have published a book and have been paid to give one seminar." If I could accomplish those two things this year, I would be well on my way to achieving my ideal future.

These are just ideas and examples. Your list is your list. You can write it how you want to. Just remember that every step is something that you would commit to doing this year and that every step would get you closer to some aspect of your vision statement.

Take a few minutes to look back at your vision statement from yesterday and choose 10 goals to accomplish this year:

The 10 Goals I Have Accomplished by:

1.

2.

3.

4.

5.

6.

7.

8.

9.

10.

Great job! I know that it isn't easy to come up with that list. It forces us to reach deep into a part of our brain that we don't exercise very often. Now we will start to refine and focus your list.

Your success and motivation greatly depend on creating a very clear vision of where you want to go and then staying focused until you get there.

This leads us directly into the second exercise, which is to **identify your top 5 goals for the next 90 days**. This takes just a second and is easier than the previous list. All you do is look at the list of 1-year goals you just completed and ask yourself:

"If I were only to accomplish five of my goals that would make the biggest impact on my life, what would they be? Which goals am I most passionate about?"

Write down those 5 goals from the above list you feel the most passionate about achieving. This is your "Definite Purpose."

My Definite Purpose

1. _____

2. _____

3. _____

4. _____

5. _____

Well done! This step is important because you have now taken your complete vision for your life and boiled it down to the 5 most important, most impactful goals that can change your life in a matter of weeks. These 5 goals represent the achievements that will bring you the greatest happiness in your life. You have found your "**definite purpose**!"

You will write out these 5 goals every day for the rest of this program and hopefully every day thereafter until you have accomplished them.

Your definite purpose is your main objective for the next few months. It should represent the most important accomplishments that you want for yourself. If there is anything on this list that you only feel a little bit excited about accomplishing, replace it with something you can feel passionate about. The idea is that if you could accomplish these items in the next 3 months, you would feel incredibly successful.

As it says above, you will write these 5 goals every day. There is something magical about writing these goals daily. They begin to transfer into your subconscious brain, which starts working on them without you even realizing it. We become what we think about most often. When our thoughts are focused on high achievement, it begins to manifest in our actions. Your confidence level goes up because your brain will start to act as though you are already successful and already have achieved all of these great things.

ACTION ITEMS

Every morning after writing your "definite purpose", you will write one action item to accomplish *that day* to bring you closer to that goal. For example: If one of your definite purpose items was, "I spend quality time every day with my family", then one of your action steps for the day might be, "Take the family for ice cream after dinner." If you can complete similar action steps over a period of time, you will soon be able to truly say, "I spend quality time with my family every day."

On the next page is an example of the process you will go through every morning.

EXAMPLE

Write your Definite Purpose with daily action goals.

1. _I make $20,000 a month_

   Today's Action Step: _Research on-line marketing for the business_

2. _I have published a book and been paid to lecture_

   Today's Action Step: _Finish outline for self-improvement book_

3. _I weigh 185 lbs. and have healthy eating habits_

   Today's Action Step: _Run 3 miles in the A.M. Don't eat out for lunch_

4. _I read one non-fiction book per week_

   Today's Action Step: _Go to Barnes and Noble at lunch to buy a book_

5. _I put my family first at all times_

   Today's Action Step: _Do not respond to texts or calls when spending time with the kids_

Write your "To Do" list of other tasks to get done today.

1. _Pay bills for the business_

2. _Stop by Costco to get paper towels and diapers_

3. _Call Jim to schedule appointment_

4. _Send flowers to my amazing wife_

DAY 2 WORKSHEET

YOUR DEFINITE PURPOSE

"You are never too old to set another goal or to dream a new dream."

- C.S. Lewis

Challenge: Complete the list of 5 goals that reflect your "definite purpose". Write them down <u>every day</u>. Write them in the present tense. For example, "I make $ _____ a month" or "I show gratitude to everyone around me" or "I weigh _____." Your daily action steps should consist of tasks you can complete <u>today</u> to get closer to achieving your definite purpose.

Definite Purpose

1. _____

Today's Action Step: _____

2. _____

Today's Action Step: _____

3. _____

Today's Action Step: _____

4. _____

Today's Action Step: _____

5. _____

Today's Action Step: _____

Other Daily Tasks (To Do List):

1. _____

2. _____

3. _____

4. _____

Evening Follow-Up

What are three things I did well today?

1. _____

2. _____

3. _____

What could I have done better?

_____

_____

_____

Thoughts from the Day

DAY 3

DATE: _____

THE LAW OF ATTRACTION

Here we are on the third day of this exciting process. Hopefully you have already started to notice some changes in the way you think and maybe even the way you act. Today we will talk about an exciting principle that will help you start to feel the results of your efforts. It is called the **Law of Attraction.**

The Law of Attraction was first described in the 1800's but was made most popular in 2006 with the release of the DVD and book, *The Secret.* The Law of Attraction says that our thoughts (both conscious and subconscious) can affect things in the outside world. We draw to ourselves the things we think about most often. **Like attracts like.**

How could this work? One theory is called "Creative Visualization." The idea is this:

1. All of our thoughts and brainwaves are made up of energy.
2. Everything in the world is made up of tiny energy particles grouped together.
3. Energy can be affected by other forms of energy.
4. Thought energy can organize matter energy.
5. Therefore, what we focus our thoughts on, we can create or attract to us.

What does this mean? The idea is that your thoughts have a power that ripples out into the universe and attracts to you those things that will help you to be successful. You will draw to you those things that will help you to achieve your goals. Sounds kind of crazy right? I thought so too, until I tried it.

One day I wrote down a goal to become a more grateful person. During the day I thought of ways to have more gratitude. In the afternoon I was looking through past e-mails in search of a certain correspondence. I came upon an e-mail I had never opened with the subject reading: "Thought you might like this." So I opened it and downloaded the attachment. It was a worksheet called "The Attitude of Gratitude". It was a way to develop deeper gratitude in one's personal life. Coincidence? Maybe. But to me it felt like a small miracle. I have had dozens of similar experiences in the past year as I applied the Law of Attraction in my life. Just ask me how often I get front row parking at a busy shopping mall or movie theater. Every time.

You will notice the same thing. As soon as you have developed a vision of your future and start setting personal goals, events will present themselves in your life that will aid you in the attainment of those goals. If you keep your eyes open, you will notice them happening more and more often. **Before long, it will seem like the whole universe is conspiring to make you successful!**

Now, is this really some magical force? No. But it will feel like it. It is like when you buy a new green Toyota and then magically the next day it seems like everybody in the world bought a green Toyota. You see them everywhere! Are there really more of them? No. But you have become sensitive to seeing green Toyotas so it feels like a conspiracy! When you set new goals for yourself, you will become more sensitive to those things around you that will aid you in your success. If you are ready to recognize them, you will be able to take advantage of them when someone else may let them pass by, calling it "chance" or "coincidence."

A great way to visualize the Law of Attraction is to think of your self as a powerful magnet. The strength and direction of your magnetic force is determined by what you focus on and how strongly you focus on it. As you focus on what you want, you will attract those things that will aid in achieving your goal. It is like running a magnet over a pile of metal filings. The small metal pieces attract to the magnet. If you focus on positive thoughts and experiences, you will attract positive things into your life. But be careful because it works both ways. If you create a negative charge through negative thinking, you will attract negativity into your life.

The Law of Attraction doesn't care what you want; it reacts to what you focus on. So the phrase "I need more money" makes you continue to "need more money". If you want to change this you would focus your thoughts on the goal (having more money) rather than the problem (needing more money). This might take the form of phrases such as "I will make more money" or "I will find a job that pays very well". Instead of "I don't want to be sick", you would say, "I live a healthy life."

Focus on the desired result instead of the current problem.

This is why I ask you to write your goals in the present tense. When you write them as though you have already obtained them, you send out the positive magnetic force that will draw those opportunities to you.

As you start to shift your focus onto the positive things you want in life, you will notice the small ways in which the universe will put the right opportunities in your path. Watch for these small occurrences. Use them to reinforce your new habits and push you to continue on. The stronger your goals and desire to attain them, the more you will notice the Law of Attraction coming to work for you. It truly will seem like a miracle when it happens.

DAY 3 WORKSHEET

THE LAW OF ATTRACTION

"You create your own universe as you go along."

- Winston Churchill

Challenge: Now that you have set your "definite purpose" and you are making a daily action plan to achieve that purpose, keep your eyes open for the many ways in which your thoughts, desire, and determination will seem to make the world work in your favor.

Definite Purpose

1. _____

Today's Action Step: _____

2. _____

Today's Action Step: _____

3. _____

Today's Action Step: _____

4. _____

Today's Action Step: _____

5. _____

Today's Action Step: _____

Other Daily Tasks (To Do List):

1. _____
2. _____
3. _____
4. _____

Evening Follow-Up

What are three things I did well today?

1. _____
2. _____
3. _____

What could I have done better?

_____

_____

_____

Thoughts from the Day

DAY 4

DATE: _____

THE LAW OF ACCOUNTABILITY

"He that is good for making excuses is seldom good for anything else."

- Benjamin Franklin

The Law of Accountability says: You are accountable for the choices you make and therefore all of the results of those choices. That means all of your successes and failures. They are the result of your own choices. You must accept them good or bad. You can't change what you can't acknowledge.

I have a conversation about accountability with my son almost once a week. He'll be goofing around with his friends and I'll catch him doing something he knows he shouldn't be doing. When I talk to him about it he always says the same thing, "Austin made me do it!" So I take the opportunity to talk about accountability and taking responsibility for our own actions. As adults, we tend to do the same thing but in different words:

"My friends made me do it."

"I'm this way because of the way my parents raised me."

"I was happy until I married him/her."

"I don't have a drinking problem!"

"I'm always late because I have to drive so far to work."

"That's just who I am so don't try to change me."

"I just don't have time."

"I can't succeed because my boss is an idiot."

They all boil down to the same thing: excuses for the actions we aren't proud of. We are deferring the accountability to someone else. A distorted sense of accountability is manifested in any number of excuses or depressing thoughts. It is natural for us to want to put the blame on other people or circumstances rather than ourselves. This is called **perceptual defense**.

Perceptual defense is the mechanism our brain puts into place to defend our self-esteem. It is the system that keeps us from saying, "I'm in this situation because of my bad decisions. I am not a good manager of my life. I'm a failure." Perceptual defense is a great tool because it keeps us from getting depressed and down on ourselves.

The problem with perceptual defense is that it can blind us to the poor decisions we are making. It keeps us from being accountable for our actions. It is trying to protect our self-esteem but it is sabotaging our success. It keeps us from identifying the warning signs that are telling us we need to change.

We have to be willing to ask ourselves tough questions and be willing to give ourselves brutally honest answers. If we can't be totally honest and real with ourselves, we won't be able to progress. Acknowledgement is a very truthful conversation we have with ourselves about what we are doing, not doing, or putting up with in our life that is destructive. Acknowledgement is dealing with the truth.

So how do we "be honest with ourselves?" Here is what has worked for me:

1. Look at your life and find the areas where you don't feel totally successful.
    a. Relationships: family, friends, co-workers, neighbors etc.
    b. Work: Income, job satisfaction, progress.
    c. Recreation: How do I spend my free time?
    d. Time-management: Am I productive or just busy?
    e. Religion: Am I doing what I should be doing?
2. Identify why you aren't totally happy with your results in that area.
3. Identify the actions you have taken that have led to those results.

For example: I often complain about not having enough time to do the things that I know would make me more successful. After thinking about it, I realized that I must not be efficient with my time. So I started keeping track. Yesterday alone I spent 30 minutes browsing the Internet and almost 2 hours playing a video game. So who is to blame for my "lack of time?" Me. I spent 2 and a half hours on activities of almost no value. If I can recognize that I am the problem and take responsibility for improving my time management, I can start to improve on it. I can be 2.5 hours closer to my goals than I would have been without ever recognizing the problem.

Once you have discovered the areas that aren't working and you've identified your role in causing it, you are ready to take action. Accountability will set you up for decisive action.

If you know that your past actions have caused unsuccessful situations, you will also know that your future actions can create successful situations. Nothing happens by accident. Everything is the result of action.

Good or bad, we are where we are because we decided to be there. You have to own it. That means you own both the successes and the failures. You are in control. Be proud of yourself for all of the good things you have done. Be optimistic that you will be able to improve upon the failures. Be brave enough to have that honest talk with yourself about how things are really going. Be aware that nothing is permanent. If you like where you are, you have to keep doing what you have been doing to stay there. If you don't like where you are, you can change it.

Starting today.

DAY 4 WORKSHEET

THE LAW OF ACCOUNTABILITY

"It is easy to dodge our responsibilities, but we cannot dodge the consequences of dodging our responsibilities."

- Sir Josiah Stamp

Challenge: Think about some of your successes and failures in life and try to identify the good or bad decisions that led to them. Every result was preceded by an action of one kind or the other.

Definite Purpose

1. _____

Today's Action Step: _____

2. _____

Today's Action Step: _____

3. _____

Today's Action Step: _____

4. _____

Today's Action Step: _____

5. _____

Today's Action Step: _____

Other Daily Tasks (To Do List):

1. _____
2. _____
3. _____
4. _____
5. _____

Evening Follow-Up

Step 1: What are three things I did well today?

1. _____
2. _____
3. _____

Step 2: What could I have done better?

_____

_____

Thoughts from the Day

DAY 5

THE LAW OF BELIEF

Many of us who grew up watching Saturday Night Live in the nineties remember the sketch of Stuart Smalley looking into a mirror saying, "I deserve good things. I am entitled to my share of happiness. I refuse to beat myself up. I am an attractive person. I am fun to be with. I'm going to do a terrific show today! And I'm gonna help people! Because I'm good enough, I'm smart enough, and, doggonit, people like me!"

It is funny to watch somebody talking to himself in a mirror but what Stuart Smalley was doing is actually a very powerful technique called "auto-suggestion", "self-suggestion", or "positive affirmation". It has been used by some of the greatest achievers in the world for centuries. In fact, it may be one of the most important principles taught in this book. Let's see how it works.

The average person processes over 60,000 separate thoughts per day, of which 90% occur subconsciously. Automatic thoughts are produced by our subconscious mind and continue to execute without the involvement of our conscious mind. For example, we don't have to consciously think about making our heart beat, or taking a breath. Think about how many other things you just do, day in day out, without even consciously thinking about it. These automatic thoughts are like mini computer programs in our subconscious minds. **They automatically come into action as a response to stimuli in our environment.** These automatic thoughts determine your thought patterns, attitudes and behaviors.

Subconscious Thought Is The Root of Undesirable Actions

While many automatic thoughts are positive, some of them can create undesirable limitations in terms of your ability to evolve, progress and reach significant personal goals in your life – you could call them "success blockers". They simply prevent you from progressing in areas where you'd like to succeed.

Ask yourself, how many people you know, maybe including yourself, who despite honest attempts to change their destiny, still:

- Lead unfulfilled or unsatisfying lives
- Feel like they're not where they would like to be at this point in their lives
- Continue to struggle with money problems
- Suffer from low self confidence
- Are not satisfied with their work
- Have not found the right partner
- Are unable to lose weight
- Can't seem to get rid of destructive habits and addictions

Why do these people continue to fail? In most cases it isn't for lack of trying or desire. It's because our brains are still programmed to subconsciously react a specific way and therefore produce a certain action or behavior. Maybe seeing somebody smoking starts a cascade of subconscious thought where the person starts to crave a cigarette of their own, then they reach in their pocket, then they light a cigarette.

I have encountered another example while writing this book. When I decide to write, I get out my laptop and sit on the couch. But opening my laptop starts a cascade in my brain that leads me to automatically click on the Internet browser icon. When the Internet window is up, I automatically click on the link to check my e-mail. After checking e-mail, I start clicking through my other bookmarked links. Thirty minutes later, I haven't written a single word in the book, which was the reason I got the computer out in the first place. It is so frustrating when I realize the time I wasted when I could have been achieving my original purpose. But that is the pathway that has been created in my brain. Open laptop → click Internet browser icon → click the link to my e-mail → click through the bookmarked pages. It has happened over and over for years and now it is a tough habit to change.

Subconscious thought can be seen as a flowing river. When a river first forms it is small and can easily have its course changed by a small dam of sticks and rocks. Over a period of time it grows in size and intensity as more water fills it. Before long, the strong and continuous flow of the water carves a deep path or canyon. And it is nearly impossible to change the course of a river running through a deep canyon.

These brain pathways happen for both good and bad actions. If we write in a journal every day when we wake up for an entire month, at the end of the month it will be hard to wake up and go eat breakfast without writing in our journal first. If we train ourselves to set goals every day, before long the desire to set goals will be so strong that our entire day will feel incomplete if we didn't get it done. And imagine how successful a person could become by setting goals every day!

The power of subconscious thinking is greater than that of our conscious thinking. If our conscious mind tries to initiate a behavioral change that conflicts with the subconscious mind's pre-programmed thought patterns, **the subconscious mind always wins**. We can change our actions for a short time, but if we don't change our subconscious thinking, we will always fall back to our old habits and decisions. This is why gym membership triples every January and then falls to normal levels by April. Our New Year's resolutions are our conscious mind trying to make a change, but our subconscious mind is still stuck in the same patterns that hold us back.

You Can Make Your Subconscious Work for You

Our objective is to create powerful, positive subconscious thoughts that will go to work for you without you even thinking about it. This is where the principle of autosuggestion comes into play. If we think certain thoughts every day, over a short period of time our brain will learn them, believe them, and change our behavior so that we fulfill them. Here is how you do it.

Start by listing all of the qualities that you wish you possessed in your life. Write them down in the present tense as though you already possess these qualities. For example:

- I am happy and healthy.
- I succeed at anything I work hard at.
- I am kind to all those I meet.
- I am getting wealthier each day.
- I study and comprehend quickly.
- I am calm and relaxed in every situation.
- My thoughts are under my control.
- Everything is getting better every day.
- I am efficient with my time.
- I show gratitude for everything in my life.

The list can be as long or short as you want. The important point is that they are statements that you really want for yourself. The stronger you desire them, the more effective it will be.

Once you have your list, your job is to take time every morning and every night to read through it. If you can do it out loud it is even better. If you can read it out loud while looking into a mirror, even better yet. The effectiveness comes from repeating it every morning and every night before going to sleep.

Why This Works

Some of you are reading this and thinking to yourself, "What did I get myself into?" It may seem awkward at first but it is essential that you start doing this if you want to bring about rapid and remarkable results in your life.

After a few days, these thoughts will soak into your subconscious and form their own pathways in your brain. So when you sit down at your computer to complete a specific task, your subconscious brain will repeat, "I am efficient with my time" and you will move directly to the task at hand without thinking twice. It is all about redirecting that river so that it flows in a positive direction.

Any criticism that comes your way, your subconscious brain will say, "That's not true. That person doesn't really know me because actually I am happy and healthy. I succeed at the things I work hard at. I am...etc." Negative comments or discouraging thoughts will fall right off of you because you have built yourself up with a positive self-image day after day.

This technique is powerful. It is the most powerful principle you will learn in this book. If you are dedicated to doing it every day, you will notice amazing results within the first week. And after a full month you will be happier, more focused and bullet-proof.

As you make your list: 1) remember that these are all qualities that you really want to claim for yourself, and 2) write them as though you already possess them. ie "I am......", "I have.....", "I do......"

Use the following page to fill in your "Positive Affirmation List."

The Qualities I Possess:

1.

2.

3.

4.

5.

6.

7.

8.

9.

10.

From here on out, this list will be known as your "**Affirmations List**." You will have the opportunity to read through it twice per day so keep this page bookmarked!

DAY 5 WORKSHEET

THE LAW OF BELIEF

"All that we are is the result of all we have thought."

- Buddha

Challenge: Make a written list of all of the qualities you would like to possess in life. Review them every morning at the start of your day and every evening before going to sleep. Reading them out loud will make them more effective.

Step 1: Read Your Affirmations List

Step 2: Write your Definite Purpose with daily action goals

1. _____

Today's Action Step: _____

2. _____

Today's Action Step: _____

3. _____

Today's Action Step: _____

4. _____

Today's Action Step: _____

5. _____

Today's Action Step: _____

Step 3: Write your "To Do" list of other tasks to get done today

1. _____
2. _____
3. _____
4. _____
5. _____
6. _____
7. _____
8. _____

Evening Follow-Up

Step 1: What are three things I did well today?

1. _____
2. _____
3. _____

Step 2: What could I have done better?

_____

_____

Step 3: Read your "Affirmations List"

Thoughts from the Day

DAY 6

DATE: _____

THE LAW OF ACTION

"Today we will do what others won't, so tomorrow we can do what others can't"

- Author Unknown

Today we will learn about the Law of Action. The Law of Action states simply that: **Life rewards action.** It can be further defined this way:

1. When we act, we see results.
2. When we act more often, we see greater results more quickly.
3. The magnitude of our results is directly proportional to the level and frequency of our action.

Seems pretty simple and obvious right? It is. But for some reason, most of us don't take advantage of this law. We have the vision in our mind of what we want our life to be, but we don't force ourselves to take action. This book is designed to help you identify your major life goals and then to do something every day to move towards those goals.

In my office I have a quote on the wall that says, "Act or be acted upon." What this means is that every day we can choose to take action and go after what we want in life, or we can choose inaction and let life happen to us. If we choose to let life happen to us, we cannot complain about our circumstances. If we act, we can take credit for all of the good results.

Can action lead to bad circumstances? Of course it can. Action works both ways. Positive action is rewarded with positive circumstances. Negative action is rewarded with negative circumstances. The difference is how your action is directed. That is why we developed your vision statement and your definite purpose in the first two days. **Your vision is both the compass and the barometer that direct and**

measure your actions. Any action that takes you closer to achieving your vision is good; anything that doesn't is a distraction.

Recently I have read a number of books about talent, genius and child prodigies. My favorite is *Outliers* by Malcom Gladwell. The most remarkable fact about most geniuses or prodigies is that they started out just like the rest of us. How can that be? The truth is that most of these people weren't born with an amazing, natural ability to perform. At a very young age they developed a great *desire* to perform. That desire led them to practice, rehearse and study longer and harder than everybody else. They decided to act. Most of them did it because they received an increase in love and praise from their parents when they performed well. Whether its Mozart, Einstein, Michael Jordan, whoever. Nobody came out of the womb automatically amazing at anything. It all comes from action. Focused and repeated action.

You can become a "prodigy" or a "genius" in just about any field you wanted to. You were born with that ability tucked down inside you. It will take an enormous effort, but I am convinced that life looks at our efforts and rewards them according to what we put in.

Most studies show that you can be the best in your field, whatever it is, if you can spend 10,000 hours studying about it. That goes for anything in life. You could be the foremost authority in the world on any topic if you could put in 10,000 hours working on it. It has been studied and replicated over and over again. Start today!

We put in the effort today so that we can be rewarded in the future. Olympic athletes will train for thousands of hours in order to be able to perform in a 10 second race. We have to take action and put in the effort if we are to expect any results. We have no claim on success unless we have put in the time and effort required to merit that success. Start today!

"Most people stand at the harbor of life waiting for their ship to come in, knowing in their heart, it never set sail."

– Krish Danham

At any moment
I could start being a better person...
But, which moment should I choose?

~ Ashleigh Brilliant

DAY 6 WORKSHEET

THE LAW OF ACTION

"I have been impressed with the urgency of doing. Knowing is not enough; we must apply. Being willing is not enough; we must do."

- Leonardo da Vinci

Challenge: The "perfect" time to act will never come. The time to act is now. Look for opportunities to take immediate action on your goals. Without action, there is no reward. Be bold and take the step.

Step 1: Read Your Affirmations List

Step 2: Write your Definite Purpose with daily action goals

1. _____

Today's Action Step: _____

2. _____

Today's Action Step: _____

3. _____

Today's Action Step: _____

4. _____

Today's Action Step: _____

5. _____

Today's Action Step: _____

Step 3: Write your "To Do" list of other tasks to get done today

1. _____
2. _____
3. _____
4. _____
5. _____
6. _____
7. _____
8. _____

Evening Follow-Up

Step 1: What are three things I did well today?

1. _____
2. _____
3. _____

Step 2: What could I have done better?

_____

_____

Step 3: Read your "Affirmations List"

Thoughts from the Day

DAY 7

DATE: _____

THE LAW OF VARIABLE PERCEPTION

"We see the world, not as it is, but as we are."

- Talmud

The Law of Perception says that no matter what happens to you in your life, the way you interpret that event and it's meaning is up to you. I added the word "variable" because everybody in the world perceives events differently. Hence the phrase, "beauty is in the eye of the beholder." You may look at something and say it is amazing while I look at it and think it is a piece of junk. We are looking at the same thing but have a totally different perception of it.

Dr. Phil McGraw once said, "There is no good news and there is no bad news. There is only news. You have the power to choose your perceptions in every circumstance, every day of your life. The key point is that you have the ability to choose differently than how you are currently choosing, if you wish."

If you picked up the newspaper one day and it said, "Phoenix Suns win the NBA Championship!" you might think it is great news. But if you were a Celtics fan you would think it was terrible news. It isn't either. It is just news. But our perceptions are different.

Our perception of the world is unique to us. No two people will ever look at an event the exact same way. Our personal perceptions are influenced by our history, personalities, points of view, etc. Steven Covey described it this way:

"Each of us tends to think we see things as they are, that we are objective. But this is not the case. We see the world, not as it is, but as we are—or, as we are conditioned to see it. When we open our mouths to describe what we see, we in effect describe ourselves, our perceptions, our paradigms. When other people disagree with us, we immediately think something is wrong with them. But, sincere, clearheaded people see things differently, each looking through the unique lens of experience."

Those factors that determine our perceptions are called filters. We all develop our filters over our lifetime. If your brother was killed by a drunk driver, you develop a filter for the way you look at all alcoholics. If you grew up in Seattle, you have a filter for how you feel about rainy days. I guarantee it is different than how an Arizonan feels about a rainy day. Our collection of filters will determine the way we look at the entire world. Filters are the reason why some people seem so optimistic and others seem so pessimistic.

When an event occurs, the way we describe it says more about us than it does about the actual facts of the event. I read a quote as a teenager that I have loved ever since:

Two men looked out from prison bars
One saw mud, the other saw stars.

Both men are in prison and looking out at the same scene before them. One of them says to himself, "Hey, I can't get any lower. It is all up from here." The other one looks out and says to himself, "This is who I am and this is who I always will be. I'm a criminal and I'm worthless." Same circumstance, different perception.

We all have the ability to choose how we will perceive and react to events in our life. Life is neutral. Our perception of it is not. It is as good or as bad as we want it to be. We can look at the world and say, "Bad things always happen to me. I always have such bad luck." Or we can look at the world and say, "I am so blessed. Great things always happen to me."

The amazing reality is that our perception creates our reality. The person who always claims to have bad luck, amazingly has more "bad luck." The person who claims to have good luck, seems to always win raffles and lotteries and door prizes. We all know that guy who always seems to have things work out for them. They are usually the ones with big dreams and ambitions. Amazingly, opportunities seem to fall into their lap.

Winston Churchill said, "We create our own universe as we go along." I have found this to be an incredibly true statement. We get to decide every day if it will be a great day or if it will be a horrible day. If we decide in the morning that the day will be great and only good things will happen to us, it will come true. Not because amazing things will happen but because we will put a positive filter on every event that comes our way.

Make that choice, every day. Decide that each day will be one of the best days of your life. Tell yourself that only good things will happen today. And as you go through the events of your day, look for ways in which every event or circumstance will make your day even better. Life was made for living and it was made for living happily. Go live it!

DAY 7 WORKSHEET

THE LAW OF VARIABLE PERCEPTION

"Life is the movie you see through your own unique eyes. It makes little difference what's happening out there. It's how you take it that counts."

- Dr. Dennis Waitley

Challenge: Tell yourself at the start of each day that this will be the best day of your life. Consider how you view daily events and look for ways to see another point of view that may be opposite your own.

Step 1: Read Your Affirmations List

Step 2: Write your Definite Purpose with daily action goals

1. _____

Today's Action Step: _____

2. _____

Today's Action Step: _____

3. _____

Today's Action Step: _____

4. _____

Today's Action Step: _____

5. _____

Today's Action Step: _____

Step 3: Write your "To Do" list of other tasks to get done today

1. _____
2. _____
3. _____
4. _____
5. _____
6. _____
7. _____
8. _____

Evening Follow-Up

Step 1: What are three things I did well today?

1. _____
2. _____
3. _____

Step 2: What could I have done better?

_____

_____

Step 3: Read your "Affirmations List"

Thoughts from the Day

Review of week 1

The Week in Review

Let's take a moment to look back at the 7 laws you learned during the first week of this book:

Day 1 – The Law of Vision

On the first day you developed the vision of your ideal, perfect future.

Day 2 – The Law of Definite Purpose

Next you developed your "definite purpose". This is your main focus for the next 3 months. It represents the activities that will get you closest to your vision.

Day 3 – The Law of Attraction

The Law of Attraction says that you are a human magnet and that you will attract to you those things that you focus on the most, good or bad.

Day 4 – The Law of Accountability

The Law of Accountability says that you are the only person responsible for where you are today and where you will be tomorrow. No one else.

Day 5 – The Law of Belief

The Law of Belief teaches us that what we believe, we become. You developed your "affirmations list" of qualities you want to claim for yourself and started reading it twice a day.

Day 6 – The Law of Action

The Law of Action tells us simply that life rewards action. You learned that to make bold improvements and successes, you have to take bold and decisive action.

Day 7 – The Law of Variable Perception

Finally we learned about the Law of Perception which tells us that the world is not one way or the other; it is as we interpret it. It teaches us that we can look at life as a skeptic or as an optimist and that how we see the world will determine how successful we can become.

Understanding these laws will bring you great success and happiness. They are applicable to any aspect of your life. If you feel you don't understand one, go back and reread it before moving on to the next section. In the next section we will learn principles that will help us continue applying these laws.

Thoughts from Week 1

What results have you seen in the first week? What have been the biggest obstacles to overcome?

_____

_____

_____

_____

_____

_____

_____

_____

_____

_____

_____

_____

_____

_____

_____

_____

_____

_____

_____

WEEK 2

Putting the Principles into Practice

DAY 8

SPINDLETOP

Zig Ziglar once told this great story: Toward the end of the 1800's, in a town near Beaumont, Texas there lived a retired military captain named George W. O'Brien. He had lived in the area for many years and owned some property nearby. Times were tough in the area and Captain O'Brien had struggled at a number of different vocations trying to make a living.

One day some men came to him and told him that they believed there was oil on the property he owned and they would like to drill for it. They would pay him royalties on every barrel of oil produced from the land, which was speculated to be about 50 barrels a day. Captain O'Brien agreed to the deal and together they formed the Gladys City Oil Company.

Years of frustration followed, with most members of the petroleum and geologic communities proclaiming the idea of oil in the area to be "silly nonsense." The little oil company went through numerous mechanics and drillers as they attempted to find oil. It looked to be a hopeless venture.

But on January 10th, 1901 the crew was inserting the piping into to the hole and mud started bubbling up. Then there was a rumble and the 700 feet of piping shot out of the hole. Then another rumble followed by a gush of mud, then natural gas and then oil. The oil shot up with such force that it shattered the oil derricks and sent a plume of oil 150 feet into the air. It was the biggest oil gusher ever seen in the world. It took 9 days just to get it under control and almost a million barrels of oil were lost. It became known as Spindletop, the most productive oil well in history. It didn't produce the 50 barrels a day that was initially thought. It produced nearly 100,000 barrels per day, more than all of the other producing wells in the United States **combined**!

George O'Brien became a millionaire that day. Or did he? The truth is that Captain O'Brien was a millionaire the day he came onto the land. But until they made the effort to dig down and discover the oil, go through the process of bringing it to the surface and take it out into the marketplace, the land was thought to be of no value.

Why Spindletop Matters to You

Often times we are like the story of Spindletop. There is so much value buried inside each of us. Our great task in life is to find a way to discover our value, bring it out, and put it to work. But until we do that, it is all just unrealized potential. And, to me, nothing is more frustrating than potential that just stays potential and never develops into anything greater.

We need to look inside ourselves and realize that we were each born with everything it takes to be successful and happy, no matter the circumstances around us. What is around us is nothing in comparison to what is within us. However, most people allow those external factors to keep them from ever drilling down to bring out their internal value. We let things like the economy, friendships, our family situation, our work situation, and our level of education act as excuses for not working to develop ourselves. As we talked about in the introduction, all of those excuses for not being happy are really just excuses for not wanting to put in the effort to be happy.

Remember that they first started drilling oil at Spindletop nearly 10 years before <u>any</u> oil was discovered. They failed over and over and over and they quit drilling at least 5 times only to try again. They lost millions of dollars with no results. The original partnership failed. They were laughed at by everyone who was considered an "expert" on oil drilling. But they kept drilling in that barren field and one day fortune decided that they had put in enough work and granted their greatest desire... multiplied by 1000.

Take the time to look inside and pull out your inherent strengths. You may find it hard or think that you don't have them but you do. Some of us have been so beat up by those things around us that we have forgotten our true value. We let life decide our worth. Don't do that. Let your worth decide your life. Find it, cultivate it, and bring it to the top.

"Nature cannot be tricked or cheated. She will give up to you the object of your struggles only after you have paid her price."

– Napoleon Hill

DAY 8 WORKSHEET

POTENTIAL

DATE: _____

"Lord, we may know what we are, but know not what we may be."
"To be, or not to be: that is the question."

- William Shakespeare

Challenge: Take some time to reflect on your life and look at all of the blessings and good things you already have. Look at what you have already accomplished and realize that you can, and will, accomplish much more.

Step 1: Read Your Affirmations List

Step 2: Write your Definite Purpose with daily action goals

1. _____

Today's Action Step: _____

2. _____

Today's Action Step: _____

3. _____

Today's Action Step: _____

4. _____

Today's Action Step: _____

5. _____

Today's Action Step: _____

Step 3: Write your "To Do" list of other tasks to get done today

1. _____
2. _____
3. _____
4. _____
5. _____
6. _____
7. _____
8. _____

Evening Follow-Up

Step 1: What are three things I did well today?

1. _____
2. _____
3. _____

Step 2: What could I have done better?

_____

_____

Step 3: Read your "Affirmations List"

Notes from the Day

DAY 9

DATE: _____

PAYING THE RENT

I once heard a wonderful lecture by a young man named Rory Vaden. In his lecture he shared the following thought:

"Success is never owned, it is rented; and the rent is due every day."

I really love that quote. I can't tell you how many times I have found that to be true in my life. I have had it happen repeatedly in my business life. Through hard work the office would start doing really well; and as soon as it started doing well I relaxed on the same hard work that got me there. And sure enough within a few weeks I was stressed out again because it seemed like success had escaped me. It was like a cycle.

I have also experienced the same in many aspects of my personal life. I can think of numerous diets, workout plans, friendships, and other situations that started off very successful but later faded back to their initial state because I failed to put continued effort into them.

Many of the highly successful or wealthy people you know got there through hard work and vision. There are very few who received an amazingly large inheritance and are just living off of it. Most successful people became successful and then remained successful because they never stopped working at it.

A good example of this idea is Tiger Woods. When he came onto the PGA tour he was dominant from early on. He won numerous championships. And at the height of his career, while ranked #1 in the world, he got a new golf coach and changed his swing. Why would he do that? He was already the best. But he could see areas where he could get even better. He was "paying the rent." He was paying the price for success. And it paid off. He started playing even better.

Fast-forward a couple of years. Tiger was still one of the best in the world but his hold on the #1 ranking had slipped a little. He didn't seem as dominant as he had been before. It seemed he had trouble with consistency in his golf game. Soon we all found out why. His focus had slipped to other ambitions and diversions in life. He started focusing elsewhere and forgot to "pay the rent" that was due to be the best golfer in the world. When the rent doesn't get paid, eviction from that position is soon to follow.

As you go through this program you will hit high points and low points. There will be days where you will feel like you have achieved so much and you will have days where you feel like you aren't progressing at all. The most important part of this whole book is that you do it every day. You cannot feel like being successful for one week earns you the right to miss a few days. The "rent" is due every day. Pay it and you will see the amazing results.

"It is not a great work done on a single day that creates our value and success in life. Though often going unnoticed, the steady repetition of hard work and small successes every day determines our true greatness."

- Kris Heap

DAY 9 WORKSHEET

PAY THE RENT

"A duty dodged is like a debt unpaid; it is only deferred, and we must come back and settle the account at last."

Joseph Fort Newton

Challenge: The results you have experienced so far are temporary and need to be reproduced every day. You can't say, "I met my goals, I can stop writing goals down every day." When you do that, you will see all of your results slip back to where you were before. Remember to "pay the rent!"

Step 1: Read Your Affirmations List

Step 2: Write your Definite Purpose with daily action goals

1. _____

Today's Action Step: _____

2. _____

Today's Action Step: _____

3. _____

Today's Action Step: _____

4. _____

Today's Action Step: _____

5. _____

Today's Action Step: _____

Step 3: Write your "To Do" list of other tasks to get done today

1. _____
2. _____
3. _____
4. _____
5. _____
6. _____
7. _____
8. _____

Evening Follow-Up

Step 1: What are three things I did well today?

1. _____
2. _____
3. _____

Step 2: What could I have done better?

_____

_____

Step 3: Read your "Affirmations List"

Notes from the Day

DAY 10

DATE: _____

EAT THAT FROG

"Eat a live frog first thing every morning and nothing worse will happen to you the rest of the day."

- Mark Twain

Brian Tracy wrote a classic book on time management called *Eat that Frog!* The book was based on the above quote from Mark Twain. The basic idea is this:

On any given day, you have a list of tasks you need to do. They range from important to unimportant, and from big to small. But somewhere on that list there is one task that is important, necessary, and the one you are least looking forward to doing. Most of us put that one off as long as possible because we just dread the thought of having to do it. That one is your "frog."

When we put off "eating the frog", it weighs on us all day long. We are less likely to do our other tasks because we waste so much energy worrying about the "frog." We get overwhelmed with the feeling that we have so much to do. It really wears us out.

But, if we look at our list of tasks, find the "frog" and take care of it first thing in the morning, we have an entirely different experience throughout the day. With that one out of the way, we already feel a sense of accomplishment right from the start. Every other task seems easy because we have gained momentum through-out the day. It is amazing how much less stress you will feel during the day when you start to implement this idea.

There is another benefit to doing your biggest, most important task early in the morning. It is the time of day when you are the most alert and have the most energy. The big task will be easier and you will do it better early in the day. By the time the afternoon rolls around, you are more tired and less focused because of everything else you had to do.

Here's a helpful method for identifying your "frog" that comes from Tsh Oxenreider, author of the Simple Mom Blog:

1. First, **create something that outlines your tasks for the day**. You can use a journal, a piece of scratch paper, a receipt, anything. Whatever works for you, just do *something*. Fill out a detailed to-do list for your day.

2. **Narrow down your list to ten items or less.** You shouldn't reasonably expect to do more – though if you find yourself having done ten things, you can simply add more items. By starting with a ten-item checklist, you're not as daunted, and you feel more accomplished to get seven whole things crossed off in one day. Seven out of ten is more impressive than seven out of 34.

3. Out of those ten things, **pick your three most important tasks (MIT's)**– the things you *really* need to do today; those tasks that if all you accomplished today were those three, you would consider it a successful day. Write those separately up top.

4. Out of those three things, **pick the worst one**. (That's your frog.) Do that task first before any others.

5. Out of your list of ten, **pick your favorite or easiest item**. For me, it's usually checking my e-mail. Whatever you do, make sure you *don't* do that task first. In fact, if you're daring, don't do that task *until* you get all three MIT's done. **Make doing that task your reward.** These tasks are those that you enjoy but are neither important nor urgent. Most of them aren't really tasks (ie. Facebook, E-Mail, Video Games, etc.)

Eating the Frog is one of those principles that will have an immediate effect on your life. You will notice its impact the first day you do it. Your day will just feel like it was easier and more successful. It doesn't require any more work or effort. In fact, you will feel like it took less energy.

So go ahead and find your frog every morning and eat that sucker right away. After all, if you had to eat a live frog every morning, you wouldn't want to have to look at it any longer than necessary. Just pinch your nose, close your eyes and get it done.

DAY 10 WORKSHEET

EAT THAT FROG

"Good things happen when you get your priorities straight."

- Scott Caan

Challenge: Every day, look at your list of items that need to be completed and pick out that big one that you are dreading the most. Put a star by it and get that one done first. You will be amazed at how much easier your day goes and the sense of accomplishment you will feel.

Step 1: Read Your Affirmations List

Step 2: Write your Definite Purpose with daily action goals

1. _____

Today's Action Step: _____

2. _____

Today's Action Step: _____

3. _____

Today's Action Step: _____

4. _____

Today's Action Step: _____

5. _____

Today's Action Step: _____

Step 3: Write your "To Do" list. (Locate your frog!)

1. _____
2. _____
3. _____
4. _____
5. _____
6. _____
7. _____
8. _____

Evening Follow-Up

Step 1: What are three things I did well today?

1. _____
2. _____
3. _____

Step 2: What could I have done better?

_____
_____

Step 3: Read your "Affirmations List"

Thoughts from the Day

DAY 11

DATE: _____

BY-PRODUCTS

by-product – *noun* - a secondary or incidental product deriving from a process or reaction, that is not the primary product or service being produced. A by-product can be useful and marketable or it can be considered waste.

We have all heard of by-products. They are the scraps and leftovers that we are stuck with after we make something. They can be as simple as the sawdust on the floor after making a wood cabinet or they can be as complex as the chemicals that are produced during the process of turning coal into useable energy. Almost everything we make has some kind of by-product.

Successful companies look at ways to collect the by-products of their work and turn them into something marketable. Coal companies found that the by-products of their process could be used to make concrete and drywall. Oil refineries use their by-products to make asphalt for our roads.

Every once in a while a company finds that the by-product becomes even more valuable than the initial product. Many businesses have to design an entirely new computer platform in order to bring out a new product. Those computer platforms are often times incredibly successful. During the filming of Peter Jackson's Lord of the Rings movies, over 150 new technologies and platforms were invented just to produce the effects that they wanted. Those advancements have been used in almost every major action movie since, including: *I Robot, King Kong* and *The Chronicles of Narnia* movies.

So what are the by-products in our life? What is there in our life that we have been tossing aside but could be used for our benefit? There are probably a number of things. But what I want to talk about is our <u>time.</u> Not our time in general but specifically our free time. Those 15-20 minute chunks of time in between our appointments and other responsibilities. The time spent driving from one place to another.

The time spent before going to sleep at night. If you add up all of those small chunks of time, you will find, on average, anywhere from 1-3 hours a day! That is 100 hours a month or over 1000 hours a year!

Those precious minutes are where we can make the biggest impact on our life. They are the by-products of our day. We usually let them just slip by. But if we could find a way to use those moments to improve ourselves, we would move ahead that much faster. An extra hour a day of positive thinking and work will accelerate your results and make you feel more successful, accomplished and confident.

So how do we fill those moments? Here are a few ideas. I started listening to audio books and lectures while driving in my car. In one month I finished 5 books and over 12 hours of lectures. The month before that, I hadn't read a single book! Imagine the difference in how I felt about myself and how much I learned just by filling the time that used to be filled with sports talk radio.

Here are just a few other ideas:

1. Keep a book with you during the day whether paperback or on an iPod.
2. Keep a notebook or journal with you to write down your thoughts.
3. Tackle something from your daily "To Do" list.
4. Call a friend or loved one just to talk or tell them you appreciate them.
5. Write a thank you note to someone.
6. Review your goals and brainstorm ideas of how to accomplish them.
7. Exercise. 10 minutes of walking, push-ups, Yoga, etc. can have a big impact.
8. Learn something new. There are videos online covering anything. List some things you've always wanted to know or do and learn about them.

Your free moments are the by-products of your day. You can choose to spend them however you want. Use them wisely. I know that if you can turn off the TV or the radio, get off of Facebook, stop texting for a few minutes and start filling your free time with productive activities, you will notice an amazing leap in your happiness and sense of accomplishment. You will achieve your goals faster and progress more quickly than you ever thought possible.

A great man once said, "Show me what a man thinks when he has nothing else to think, and I will tell you what kind of man he is." Similarly, show me what a person does when they have nothing else to do, and I will tell you how successful they will be. Time works on a "use it or lose it" basis. Make it work for you.

DAY 11 WORKSHEET

BY-PRODUCTS

"Much may be done in those little shreds and patches of time which every day produces, and which most men throw away."

- Julius Caesar

Challenge: During the day, keep track of how much free time you have. Think about those little 5-minute chunks of time and add them up. Then look at how you spend those chunks of time. Try using those moments to do something positive instead of something that just wastes the time.

Step 1: Read Your Affirmations List

Step 2: Write your Definite Purpose with daily action goals

1. _____

Today's Action Step: _____

2. _____

Today's Action Step: _____

3. _____

Today's Action Step: _____

4. _____

Today's Action Step: _____

5. _____

Today's Action Step: _____

Step 3: Write your "To Do" list. (Locate your frog!)

1. _____
2. _____
3. _____
4. _____
5. _____
6. _____
7. _____
8. _____

Evening Follow-Up

Step 1: What are three things I did well today?

1. _____
2. _____
3. _____

Step 2: What could I have done better?

_____

_____

Step 3: Read your "Affirmations List"

Thoughts from the Day

DAY 12

DATE: _____

HOW TO USE YOUR "BUT"

Somewhere there is an 11 year-old boy giggling after reading the title of this chapter. It sounds funny yet there is something important to be taught here. There are few words that can have a more powerful influence for good or bad on our attitude than the word "but". Let's look at some examples of 2 different ways to use your "but."

"I could have finished school but..."
"I would stop smoking but..."
"I want to spend more time with my family but..."
"I could make more money but..."
"I would go to church but..."

This is using your "but" to precede an excuse for not doing those things of real value. When you start a sentence by saying you want to do something positive and then throw in the word "but", you just tell yourself and everyone around you that you are either: (A) not in control of your own life or (B) that you aren't willing to do what is necessary to make it happen. It really doesn't even matter what comes after the "but". Once you've said it, you have already admitted defeat.

There are, however, other ways in which you can use your "but" to have a positive effect on your attitude. Here are a few:

"We lost the game tonight but..."
"We didn't make our goals this month but..."
"I lost my job today but..."
"Today was a rough day but..."

Do you see the difference? Same word; totally different effect. When your "but" is used one way it presents an excuse. When it is used the other way, it presents an opportunity. You could have the worst day of your life...**but** at least now you know not to make those mistakes again, **but** at least tomorrow will be better, **but** you still have your family. It can be used to impact your attitude in whatever way you choose.

So make it a goal today to be careful how you use your "but". Learn to make your "but" work positively for you. Your "but" could determine your success in life.

*"I am not bound to win
<u>but</u> I am bound to be true;
I am not bound to succeed
<u>but</u> am bound to live up
to what light I have."*

- Abraham Lincoln

DAY 12 WORKSHEET

USING YOUR "BUT"

"There is no such thing as a list of reasons. There is either one sufficient reason or a list of excuses."

- Robert Brault

Challenge: As you go through your day, take note of how you use your "but." Do you use it to make an excuse for not taking action, or do you use it as a stepping-stone to do better?

Step 1: Read Your Affirmations List

Step 2: Write your Definite Purpose with daily action goals

1. _____

Today's Action Step: _____

2. _____

Today's Action Step: _____

3. _____

Today's Action Step: _____

4. _____

Today's Action Step: _____

5. _____

Today's Action Step: _____

Step 3: Write your "To Do" list. (Locate your frog!)

1. _____
2. _____
3. _____
4. _____
5. _____
6. _____
7. _____
8. _____

Evening Follow-Up

Step 1: What are three things I did well today?

1. _____
2. _____
3. _____

Step 2: What could I have done better?

_____

_____

Step 3: Read your "Affirmations List"

Thoughts from the Day

DAY 13

DATE: _____

THE MASTERMIND GROUP

Mastermind Group - "A coordination of knowledge and effort, in a spirit of harmony, between two or more people, for the attainment of a definite purpose."

The mastermind was formally described for the first time by Napoleon Hill in his 1937 book, *Think and Grow Rich.* In researching his book, Hill studied the wealthiest men in the world over a 25-year period. He found that in every case he studied, the subject had used some form of "mastermind group". He went so far as to say that if you "analyze the record of any man who has accumulated a great fortune, and many of those who have accumulated modest fortunes, you will find that they have either consciously, or unconsciously employed the 'Master Mind' principle."

The idea is that a group of people who have similar goals and motivation can come together and form a kind of "super brain" or "master mind" which is greater than the sum of its parts. This is also the definition of synergy. It would be like a group of people with an IQ of 100 (average) getting together to share their collective ideas and wisdom and, in so doing, the IQ of the group is 160 (genius).

A mastermind group is developed to support each other and help one another set higher goals. Ideas and criticisms are exchanged openly in a positive way to help each member improve. Examples of mastermind groups are the President's cabinet, Alcoholics Anonymous, and church groups.

Mastermind groups can have both good and bad effects on the members. They can be organized for bad reasons. I remember scenes from movies like Dick Tracey, Austin Powers, or Batman where all of the stereotypical bad guys sitting around trying to figure out how to defeat the hero. They are a Mastermind.

You are already a part of the most common form of mastermind group in the world! Your group gets together just about every day and the issues you focus on decide your daily actions as well as your future success and happiness. Without knowing it you have formed your own group of like-minded individuals. Your mastermind group is also called "friends".

Believe it or not, your actions reflect the values and ideals of the friends that surround you. Big surprise right? But it is more true than you might think. If you spend enough time with people who drink alcohol excessively, you will eventually begin to drink as much as they do. If you spend a majority of your time around people who are negative or criticize others, you will start to have that same negative attitude about life. If you are surrounded by losers, guess what, you are on the road to becoming a loser. It isn't a maybe; it is a definite. You will become like the people that surround you. Surround yourself with positive, happy, successful people so you can be like that.

The benefits of having a supportive mastermind group are plenty:

1. You have a group of people available to help you succeed.
2. You get the benefit of differing perspectives, input and feedback.
3. Your mastermind team can bring resources and connections to the table you might not have come up with on your own.
4. You receive accountability and inspiration from the group, thus enabling you to maintain focus in achieving your goals.

Napoleon Hill even went so far as to say there was a mystical quality created when a mastermind group was formed. He said: "No two minds ever come together without, thereby, creating a third, invisible, intangible force which may be likened to a third mind."

In other words, your ability to create things in the world is increased by having that invisible "third mind" of the mastermind group.

You'd be surprised at how willing many people are to help you when asked. People feel that it is an honor to be asked for advice or an opinion. You don't necessarily need to meet with your entire team in person in a formal setting. You might chat with each individually on the phone, set up an email discussion list, or just go to lunch.

Finally, don't forget that your friends and family can become a mastermind support system for you. (Unfortunately, the reverse is also true: negative friends and family can equally drag you down, so be careful.) If you don't have the time to start or join a formal mastermind group, you might be lucky enough to find a good friend to share your successes with. These are friends who unconditionally support you and aren't covertly blocking your progress because of their own jealousies and insecurities. Such friends are hard to find sometimes, but if you can get one, consider yourself quite lucky.

Choose wisely who you associate with. Your actions will most likely fall in line with the people you spend time with. Look to be around people you admire and who have achieved some of the goals you are working on. Just by being around them, you will start to behave in a way that will help you achieve those goals as well.

DAY 13 WORKSHEET

THE MASTERMIND

"Alone we can do so little. Together we can do so much."

- Hellen Keller

Challenge: Take a minute to evaluate your current mastermind groups (friends, family, co-workers, etc.). Think about whether they bring you down, keep you in the same place, or make you want to be better. If your mastermind group isn't helping you progress, think about adding a new one.

Step 1: Read Your Affirmations List

Step 2: Write your Definite Purpose with daily action goals

1. _____

Today's Action Step: _____

2. _____

Today's Action Step: _____

3. _____

Today's Action Step: _____

4. _____

Today's Action Step: _____

5. _____

Today's Action Step: _____

Step 3: Write your "To Do" list. (Locate your frog!)

1. _____
2. _____
3. _____
4. _____
5. _____
6. _____
7. _____
8. _____

Evening Follow-Up

Step 1: What are three things I did well today?

1 _____
2. _____
3. _____

Step 2: What could I have done better?

_____

_____

Step 3: Read your "Affirmations List"

Thoughts from the Day

DAY 14

DATE: _____

"FAILURE"

"That which we persist in doing becomes easier. Not that the task itself has become easier, but that our ability to perform it has increased."

- Ralph Waldo Emerson

Tommy was the youngest of seven children. His father was exiled from his country for rebellious activity. Tommy only had 3 months of official schooling because his mind wandered and the teacher told his parents that he was not smart enough for school. Today we call his behavior "Attention Deficit Disorder (ADD)". Illness and infection at a young age left him partially deaf. His family fell on hard times and Tom had to sell candy and newspapers on a train in order to support the family. He found that he could supplement his income by selling vegetables. In his spare time he would sit between the boxcars and read books about philosophy and business. He learned that hard work and a little creativity could lead to bigger accomplishments. So he went to work trying to create things that "serve others". He worked hard for many years but **failed** more than any person I have ever heard of. Yet today he is known the world over. Universities, cities, and businesses are all named after that disadvantaged boy who was not smart enough for school. You know him as Thomas Edison.

Thomas Edison is widely regarded as one of the greatest men in the history of man's progress. His inventions were not only numerous but drastically improved the world. Among his inventions are the light bulb, electricity generating stations, the phonograph, the motion picture projector, and hundreds more. He was the face of the Industrial Revolution and his inventions earned him the name, "The Wizard of Menlo Park." He may have accomplished more for the technological progress of mankind than any person in history. In his lifetime, Thomas Edison truly changed the world. Most people think he was just born brilliant.

How did he do it? He failed better than other people. You see, Thomas Edison took out almost 1100 different patents for all of his ideas. Of those 1100, you have maybe heard about 10 of them at best. So what happened to the rest of them? They didn't work out. He made some things that nobody wanted or somebody else made them better. And the products that were his biggest successes didn't come easily. He failed approximately 10,000 times before he could make the light bulb work efficiently. How did he do it? He failed his way forward and didn't give up. Imagine how different history would have been if he had stopped trying after 9,999 attempts.

How did he fail so well? When his experiment didn't work the first time, Edison made a note of exactly what he'd done and what components he had used. Then he made an adjustment to the experiment and tried again. And when that "failed" he made a note of that, readjusted and tried again. He kept learning from every experiment. He learned all the ways that it wouldn't work. He discovered all the chemicals and elements that wouldn't work. Each time he found a way that wouldn't work, he knew he was closer to finding a way that would work. There was a lot of learning to go through. Nobody had done it before. He couldn't read a book about it. He simply had to plug away, failing and learning, until he and his team worked out the right way to do it.

All through his life Thomas Edison extolled the virtues of hard work and attributed many of his successes to his ability to fail and try again. I would venture to say that there has never been any great accomplishment in history that didn't first have some form of failure preceding it. We have no reason to expect that the path to our goals and ambitions won't be littered with bumps, obstacles and failures. So if we are going to achieve our goals, we better find a way to accept failure as an event, learn from it and move on to the next one.

Failure is something that happens to a person, not something that defines a person. You only fail if you don't get back up and move forward. As long as we learn from each failure and do something a little different the next time, we will fail our way to the top. Remember: If you fail, fail forward.

"Many of life's failures are people who did not realize how close they were to success when they gave up."

- Thomas Edison

DAY 14 WORKSHEET

FAILURE

"Many of life's failures are people who did not realize how close they were to success when they gave up."

- Thomas Edison

Challenge: Consider your greatest successes and accomplishments in life. Think about the struggles and small failures that accompanied those great accomplishments. As you work on your daily goals, don't get discouraged if you fail or miss a day. Just pick yourself up and start again.

Step 1: Read Your Affirmations List

Step 2: Write your Definite Purpose with daily action goals

1. _____

Today's Action Step: _____

2. _____

Today's Action Step: _____

3. _____

Today's Action Step: _____

4. _____

Today's Action Step: _____

5. _____

Today's Action Step: _____

Step 3: Write your "To Do" list. (Locate your frog!)

1. _____
2. _____
3. _____
4. _____
5. _____
6. _____
7. _____
8. _____

Evening Follow-Up

Step 1: What are three things I did well today?

1. _____
2. _____
3. _____

Step 2: What could I have done better?

_____

_____

Step 3: Read your "Affirmations List"

Thoughts from the Day

Review of week 2

Week 2 In Review

You've made it through another week! Week 2 was designed to give you a few supplemental principles to help fill in some of the gaps or maybe just to give you a boost. Let's review them briefly:

Day 8 – Spindeltop (Potential)
We used the story of the oil discovery at Spindeltop as a metaphor for the hidden potential within us. If we don't find a way to bring it out, it is worthless.

Day 9 – Pay the Rent
We learned that success is never owned, it is rented; and the rent is due every day. We have to put in an effort every day to obtain and maintain success. That means continuing to set goals and take action steps every day.

Day 10 – Eat That Frog
In this section we learned how to locate that one task that we are dreading for the day and which is causing us the most stress. We have to get that one done first so we can have a much less stressful day.

Day 11 – By-products
We talked about utilizing the small chunks of spare time in our day to work towards our goals. We have a lot more time in the day than we realize!

Day 12 – Using your "But"
The way we use a simple three-letter word can make all the difference in how we look at life. This ties in with the Law of Variable Perception.

Day 13 – The Mastermind Group
A wonderful way to either progress or stay stagnant is to be a part of master-mind group. Some groups will push us and accelerate our results; others will hold us back. We have to evaluate which are which.

Day 14 – "Failure"
The story of Thomas Edison teaches us a lot about failure and how we view that word. It is okay to fail at something, if you learn from it and do better next time.

Week 3 is a series of examples of how great people have used these laws and principles to succeed.

Thoughts from Week 2

WEEK 3

Persistence in the Practice of the Principles

DAY 15

DATE: _____

CROSSING THE RUBICON

On a cold January morning in 49 B.C., a young Roman general stood with his army on the banks of a small river in northern Italy called the Rubicon. This river represented the northern border of Italy proper. He stood on the banks, deep in thought, as he contemplated his next move.

He had been fighting in the service of his country in barbaric lands for 9 years with great success. In fact, his success was so great that he became one of the most popular generals in the Roman Empire.

But with great success and popularity came adversity. The leaders in Rome began to fear his popularity as a threat to their own power. So the leaders convinced the Senate that he was a danger to the peace of the Empire. The Senate sent a message to the general, commanding him to disband his army, resign his command and return to Rome as a civilian. He was by no means to cross into Italy proper at the head of an army.

What was he to do? Obey the command of the country he had served all of his life, or follow his vision of a new and different world? He was ambitious. He wanted to become the ruler of the Roman Empire. But to take that step, to cross that river, was to plunge the entire Empire into civil war.

On that decisive morning, Julius Caesar took a few steps into that frigid water, blew on a horn signaling the army to advance, and yelled, "Advance! Let us go where the Gods summon us. The die is cast!" And with that decisive move, the history of the world was changed.

To this day, the term "Crossing the Rubicon" is used when someone makes an important decision with major, life-changing implications. It signifies a decision to forget those things that are past and move on to a bold, new vision.

At some point we all have our moment to "cross the Rubicon." That moment where we are standing on the banks, looking back at where we have been and forward to a new day. Behind us is familiar territory, before us is the unknown. But the call of a better life draws us forward in spite of our uncertainties. The path ahead will not be easy but it will be worth it.

Your Rubicon may be quitting a job to focus on something you would rather do. It may be letting go of hurt feelings from the past. It could be writing the book you have always wanted to write. It could be anything that is important to you but you are hesitant to do. It is probably already on your vision statement.

Hopefully as you have worked through this book, you have been feeling more capable and confident. You have set your sights on the kind of life that will bring you happiness and fulfillment. You stand at the banks, now make the decision to move forward with boldness and faith in yourself. Today is the day that you "cross the Rubicon."

DAY 15 WORKSHEET

THE RUBICON

"As a rule, men worry more about what they can't see than about what they can."

- Julius Caesar

Challenge: What is your Rubicon? What is that fear or obstacle that has kept you from achieving your goals? Make a promise to yourself today that you will move forward without worrying about failure or defeat. Cross your Rubicon and look forward to a better day.

Step 1: Read Your Affirmations List

Step 2: Write your Definite Purpose with daily action goals

1. _____

Today's Action Step: _____

2. _____

Today's Action Step: _____

3. _____

Today's Action Step: _____

4. _____

Today's Action Step: _____

5. _____

Today's Action Step: _____

Step 3: Write your "To Do" list. (Locate your frog!)

1. _____
2. _____
3. _____
4. _____
5. _____
6. _____
7. _____
8. _____

Evening Follow-Up

Step 1: What are three things I did well today?

1. _____
2. _____
3. _____

Step 2: What could I have done better?

_____

_____

Step 3: Read your "Affirmations List"

Thoughts from the Day

DAY 16

DATE: _____

DEFYING GRAVITY

In the Broadway musical *Wicked*, the main character is named Elphaba. She is one of the most powerful young witches in the land. But she has one obstacle to overcome. She was born with green skin! And because of that, the other kids at school avoid her and shun her.

At a crucial point in the story she is forced to decide between doing what she knows is right and doing what will make her popular with the other kids. Doing the right thing will mean a great sacrifice for her and force her to step out on a limb and put her faith in her self. These are the words she sings as she decides to take that big step:

> Something has changed within me, something is not the same.
> I'm through with playing by the rules of someone else's game.
> Too late for second-guessing, too late to go back to sleep
> It's time to trust my instincts, close my eyes: and leap!
> I'm through accepting limits 'cause someone says they're so
> Some things I cannot change but 'til I try, I'll never know!
> It's time to try
> Defying gravity
> I think I'll try
> Defying gravity
> And you can't pull me down!

I've thought a lot about this song and what is symbolized by "gravity". In our lives, gravity represents all of those things that hold us back, all of those people who tell us we can't do something, and that inner voice of doubt that creeps in whenever we think of doing something great.

We have all set goals or New Year's resolutions for ourselves only to return to our old ways within a short period of time. What causes us to settle back into those habits we don't like? Gravity. Sometimes it is our own laziness. Sometimes it is our friends holding us back. Often times it is our attitude and how we see ourselves and the world around us.

Last week, we talked about using the word "but". When you say, "I want to work hard and become the best _____ in the world, BUT......." Anything you say after the "BUT" is your gravity. That is the thing holding you down and keeping you from rising up and grabbing a better future.

- But I'm not smart enough
- But my friends will laugh at me
- But my parents didn't raise me right
- But I don't know how
- But I don't have time
- But people don't see me that way
- But I'm not good enough

You may have really good excuses for not accomplishing your goals. But in the end, they are just excuses. They are your personal gravity, letting you improve a little before pulling you back down.

Your determination has to be enough to negate the effects of gravity. Try to leave behind those things that keep you tethered down. Decide that you won't let what others say or think deter you from your goal. Nothing else matters except for your resolve to live a better more fulfilling life. Look up, decide to be great, and **start defying gravity!**

What's Your Gravity?

List 5 factors that keep you from achieving your loftiest goals:

1.
2.
3.
4.
5.

DAY 16 WORKSHEET

DEFYING GRAVITY

"Gravity is one variable in a lot of scientific processes. If you can remove gravity or minimize its effect, then you can understand the processes that are really going on."

- Laurel Clark

Challenge: Take a few moments to examine your life or your personality and think about those things that are acting as the "gravity". Think about ways to overcome or remove those sources so that you can achieve your goals more quickly and more fully.

Step 1: Read Your Affirmations List

Step 2: Write your Definite Purpose with daily action goals

1. _____

Today's Action Step: _____

2. _____

Today's Action Step: _____

3. _____

Today's Action Step: _____

4. _____

Today's Action Step: _____

5. _____

Today's Action Step: _____

Step 3: Write your "To Do" list. (Locate your frog!)

1. _____
2. _____
3. _____
4. _____
5. _____
6. _____
7. _____
8. _____

Evening Follow-Up

Step 1: What are three things I did well today?

1. _____
2. _____
3. _____

Step 2: What could I have done better?

_____

_____

Step 3: Read your "Affirmations List"

Thoughts from the Day

DAY 17

DATE: _____

CRITICISM

"It is not the critic who counts: not the man who points out how the strong man stumbles or where the doer of deeds could have done better. The credit belongs to the man who is actually in the arena, whose face is marred by dust and sweat and blood, who strives valiantly, who errs and comes up short again and again, because there is no effort without error or shortcoming, but who knows the great enthusiasms, the great devotions, who spends himself for a worthy cause; who, at the best, knows, in the end, the triumph of high achievement, and who, at the worst, if he fails, at least he fails while daring greatly, so that his place shall never be with those cold and timid souls who knew neither victory nor defeat."

- Theodore Roosevelt

One of the great detractors in our path towards greatness is criticism. Even the thought of possibly being criticized for a decision is enough to keep us from ever making that decision. Criticism comes in many forms. We hear of constructive criticism but in my experience it exists in a miniscule amount when compared to destructive criticism.

We have all been criticized for decisions we have made. But I want to take a look at some of the psychology of criticism. There is a reason why some people make a living (or a well-practiced hobby) of criticizing others. It has little to do with the person being criticized and much more to do with the criticizers themselves.

Those who criticize others are really coming from a point of insecurity. They feel bad about who they are as a person. They are afraid that if people look long enough at them, they will realize that they are inadequate. So their tactic is to criticize everyone else so that others will be so busy looking at you, they won't have time to look at the failures in their own life. We have all known people like this. Often times they are the person who "knows all the gossip." They could sit around for hours talking about how someone raises their kids wrong or how somebody's marriage is in trouble or who can't afford the car they are driving. They expend an amazing amount of energy trying to shift the focus from themselves onto other people. It is their defense mechanism. They are sad and insecure and they don't want anybody to find out.

Before we put all of the blame solely on the criticizer, it should be mentioned that there would be no criticizers if there were no audiences to listen to them. We are also to blame. We like listening to those criticisms because then we feel better about ourselves. Hey, if the Jones' kid is on drugs, then it's not so bad that my kid stole money from my wallet. Probably both parents have failed somewhere along the way, but I sure feel better knowing that somebody else's kid is also making bad choices. And since we are talking about the Jones', at least they aren't talking about me.

So what should we do to avoid falling into that category? The first on our list should be to realize that everyone is trying to do what is best for themselves and their families. We all have different ways of doing it and we all make mistakes along the way, but we are all trying. So don't waste your time and energy dragging down others. In reality, we make ourselves look bad when we criticize others so much.

In the end, the critic has no friend.

It is not the critic who counts. When you start this process there will be people who will support you 100%. And there will be people who will be jealous of you because you are doing something that they wish they were doing. But because they don't want to put in the effort, they will try and get you to quit so that they can feel better about where they are. They feel like if you succeed it means that they have failed.

In many cases you could follow this truth: **The value of your goal is directly proportional to the amount of criticism you receive.** In other words, the more people tell you that you <u>can't</u> do it, the more you probably <u>should</u> do it. Nobody criticizes the person who says, "My goal is to start jogging." But you would find a great deal more who would criticize you for saying, "My goal is to compete in a marathon." If nobody is criticizing what you are doing, you probably aren't doing enough.

So learn to take criticism with grace and let it roll right off of you. Take joy in knowing that every time somebody tells you, "you can't", they are really saying, "I can't". Remember the words of Theodore Roosevelt, "It is not the critic who counts...the credit belongs to the man who is actually in the arena."

You are in the arena, you are starting to do great things in your life, don't listen to the critic.

DAY 17 WORKSHEET

CRITICISM

"Criticism is something we can avoid easily by saying nothing, doing nothing, and being nothing."

- Aristotle

Challenge: As you progress with your plans to change your life, realize that those who criticize you are doing so because they feel insecure about where they are in life. The truly successful person has no need to criticize others.

Step 1: Read Your Affirmations List

Step 2: Write your Definite Purpose with daily action goals

1. _____

Today's Action Step: _____

2. _____

Today's Action Step: _____

3. _____

Today's Action Step: _____

4. _____

Today's Action Step: _____

5. _____

Today's Action Step: _____

Step 3: Write your "To Do" list of other tasks to get done today

1. _____
2. _____
3. _____
4. _____
5. _____
6. _____
7. _____
8. _____

Evening Follow-Up

Step 1: What are three things I did well today?

1. _____
2. _____
3. _____

Step 2: What could I have done better?

_____

_____

Step 3: Read your "Affirmations List"

Thoughts from the Day

DAY 18

DATE: _____

LARRY LEGEND

In 1988 the National Basketball Association held its annual All-Star game in Chicago. On the day before the game there are a number of skills competitions like the dunk contest and the 3-point shooting contest.

In the 3-point shooting contest you are given 1 minute to shoot 25 basketballs from around the 3-point arc. They are set up at 5 stations with 5 balls each. Each made shot is worth 1 point except the final ball at each station (the "money ball"), which is worth 2 points.

The 1988 contest was the third annual contest. The winner of the previous two was again competing and his name was Larry Bird. Larry made his way through the preliminary rounds fairly easily until meeting up against Dale Ellis in the championship match.

Ellis went first and scored 15 points. It was Larry Bird's turn. As he worked his way around the arc, it became apparent that he just wasn't in rhythm. With only 2 stations to go he had just 7 points. He needed to be almost perfect in order to win. He made his next 5 shots in a row, bringing him to within 3 points of the win. As he moved to the last rack he shot ball 1...miss, he shot ball 2...miss. One more miss and it was over. Ball 3...make, then ball 4...make. One ball left; the "money ball". He picked it up, reared back and shot. The second the ball left his hand he turned, put one finger up in the air and started walking towards the winner's circle to collect his check and trophy. He didn't even watch to see the ball go in, he knew it from the second it left his hand. The world watched Larry Bird win the 1988 three-point shoot-out.

But what the world didn't see was everything that led up to that point. Nobody watched Larry Bird as a boy in French Lick, Indiana shooting baskets on his outdoor hoop in the middle of winter. Very few watched him shooting baskets in the gym in between classes and late into the night in high school. Very few know that he dropped out of college to be a trash collector for a year before being convinced to return.

The world watched him win NBA championships and "Most Valuable Player" awards. But nobody saw the thousands of hours of practice and preparation that led to those successes.

When Larry Bird let go of that ball and raised that finger in victory, it was more than a good shot. He knew it was going in because he had taken that shot a million times. He knew what it felt like to shoot a perfect shot. When the time came, his years of hard work kicked in and he performed with perfect confidence.

We have the opportunity to develop that level of confidence in ourselves if we are willing to put forth the effort every day. We do the important little things in life, like setting goals, over and over again so that when the time comes to perform, we will do it confidently. Those small habits are like little bank deposits that we put in over a long period of time. The day will come when they will pay dividends.

When the time comes to perform, we cannot expect to make a withdrawal if we have never made a deposit.

DAY 18 WORKSHEET

LARRY BIRD

"A winner is someone who recognizes his God-given talents, works his tail off to develop them into skills, and uses these skills to accomplish his goals. Push yourself again and again. Don't give an inch until the final buzzer sounds."
- Larry Bird

Challenge: Remember that there is nobody in the world who has become successful in any aspect of life without hard work and vision. We often don't see or even think about all of the time, work and determination that went into the successful person we see before us.

Step 1: Read Your Affirmations List

Step 2: Write your Definite Purpose with daily action goals

1. _____

Today's Action Step: _____

2. _____

Today's Action Step: _____

3. _____

Today's Action Step: _____

4. _____

Today's Action Step: _____

5. _____

Today's Action Step: _____

Step 3: Write your "To Do" list. (Locate your frog!)

1. _____
2. _____
3. _____
4. _____
5. _____
6. _____
7. _____
8. _____

Evening Follow-Up

Step 1: What are three things I did well today?

1. _____
2. _____
3. _____

Step 2: What could I have done better?

_____

_____

Step 3: Read your "Affirmations List"

Thoughts from the Day

DAY 19

DATE: _____

YOUR FOUR-MINUTE MILE

The Story of Roger Bannister

The story of Roger Bannister is an inspirational one. For many years it was widely believed to be impossible for a human to run a mile (1609 meters) in under four minutes. In fact, for many years, it was believed that the four-minute mile was a *physical barrier* that no man could break without causing significant damage to the runner's health, including having his heart burst from over-exertion. The achievement of a four-minute mile seemed beyond human possibility, like climbing Mount Everest or walking on the moon.

It was a windy spring day, on the 6th of May 1954. Bannister had doubts about running the race with the wind blowing and almost decided to save his energy for another day. But just minutes before the scheduled time of the race, the wind died down and Roger Bannister made the attempt. He crossed the finish line with a time of 3 minutes, 59.4 seconds, and broke through the "four minute mile" **psychological** barrier.

The breaking of the four minute mile was so significant, that is was named by Forbes as one of the greatest athletic achievements of all time. Roger Bannister was on the cover of the first edition of Sports Illustrated. What made this event even more significant was that after the four-minute barrier was broken by Bannister, **within three years, 16 other runners also cracked the four-minute mile!** Nobody had done it in thousands of years of history and all of a sudden within a few years, 17 people did it.

So what happened to the *physical* barrier that prevented humans from running the four-minute mile? Was there a sudden leap in human evolution? No. It was the *change in thinking* that made the difference. Bannister had shown that breaking the four-minute mile was possible. It was more a psychological barrier than a physical barrier. Once other runners saw that it was possible, they began to believe in their own ability to do it. Often the barriers we perceive are only barriers in our own minds.

"The man who can drive himself further once the effort gets painful is the man who will win."

-Roger Bannister

Our beliefs and mindsets limit or expand our world. We place our own limits by what we choose to believe. These beliefs influence what you attempt or choose not to attempt in life. They determine what you pay attention to, how you react to difficult situations and ultimately your attitude. Success and failure begin and end in what the mind believes is possible. Napoleon Hill said, "If your mind can conceive it and believe it, you can achieve it."

So what are your "four-minute miles"? What are the psychological limitations you have placed on yourself? Think of those times you say, "I wish I could do _____ but I'm not _____ enough." If you can dream it, it is possible. You just have to convince yourself of that. This is why I have you recite your "affirmations list" every day. It will help you convince yourself of just how great you really are.

People do amazing things every day that they never thought possible. If they can do it, so can you. Don't limit yourself. Set your goals high and go break your "four-minute mile."

"Whether you think you can or think you can't, you're right."
-Henry Ford

"The difference between the impossible and the possible lies in a person's determination."

-Tommy Lasorda

DAY 19 WORKSHEET

THE FOUR-MINUTE MILE

"We would accomplish many more things if we did not think of them as impossible"

- Vince Lombardi

Challenge: Look at the aspects of your definite purpose and ask yourself if someone else in the world has already been able to accomplish it. If somebody else has, then there is no reason why you cannot. If nobody else has, you have the unique opportunity to be the first!

Step 1: Read Your Affirmations List

Step 2: Write your Definite Purpose with daily action goals

1. _____

Today's Action Step: _____

2. _____

Today's Action Step: _____

3. _____

Today's Action Step: _____

4. _____

Today's Action Step: _____

5. _____

Today's Action Step: _____

Step 3: Write your "To Do" list of other tasks to get done today

1. _____
2. _____
3. _____
4. _____
5. _____
6. _____
7. _____
8. _____

Evening Follow-Up

Step 1: What are three things I did well today?

1. _____
2. _____
3. _____

Step 2: What could I have done better?

_____

_____

Step 3: Read your "Affirmations List"

Thoughts from the Day

DAY 20

DATE: _____

DON'T BOUNCE THE PITCH

Bravery in the Wake of a Tragedy

In October of 2001 the Arizona Diamondbacks and the New York Yankees met in the World Series. Just over a month before, the country had been through the tragedy of the Twin Towers. As the country mourned, there was debate as to whether or not the rest of the baseball season should even be played. After much deliberation, it was decided that the country needed baseball to resume.

The first two games were played in Arizona before the series turned to New York. The eyes of the entire country were on the city that was trying to heal from a disaster. The Yankees had become "America's team".

President George W. Bush was scheduled to throw the first pitch. There was great concern about the security issues surrounding the President being out in the open in the wake of a terrorist attack. But President Bush was determined to show the people that our country would not hide in the face of adversity.

As President Bush was in the tunnel preparing, Yankee captain Derek Jeter approached. "Any advice?" asked the President. "Just don't bounce the pitch," said Jeter. "They'll boo you." President Bush walked out to the mound to the roar of thunderous applause. He represented the hope of our nation. He stepped to the mound, wound up and threw a perfect strike on the outside corner of the plate.

There was a lot riding on that pitch. Would the world end if he bounced the pitch? No. But when his time came, the time when he needed to perform, with 50 million people watching, he put everything into the throw and delivered.

We have one chance at this life. One chance to make it happen. We can do whatever we want with our one chance. Let's give it everything we've got. **Don't bounce the pitch!** Don't give it a half effort. You can't afford to waste time dwelling in mediocrity. Decide to be great. Set the goals that will help you achieve your dreams and then go to work with all of your energy until your dreams become your reality.

Additional Quotes

"The question isn't who is going to let me; it's who is going to stop me. "
~ Ayn Rand

"Real leaders are ordinary people with extraordinary determination. "
~ Unknown Author

"There is no chance, no destiny, no fate, that can hinder or control the firm resolve of a determined soul."
~ Ella Wheeler Wilcox

"Obsessed is just a word the lazy use to describe dedicated."
~ Unknown Author

"Never give in! Never give in! Never, never, never, never - in nothing great or small, large or petty. Never give in except to convictions of honor and good sense."
~ Winston Churchill

DAY 20 WORKSHEET

DON'T BOUNCE THE PITCH

"We shall neither fail nor falter; we shall not weaken or tire...give us the tools and we will finish the job."

- Winston Churchill

Challenge: Go about your day doing everything you can to the best of your ability. Don't settle for a mediocre result. Give it everything you've got so that at the end of the day you won't be able to say, "I wish I had tried harder or done better."

Step 1: Read Your Affirmations List

Step 2: Write your Definite Purpose with daily action goals

1. _____

Today's Action Step: _____

2. _____

Today's Action Step: _____

3. _____

Today's Action Step: _____

4. _____

Today's Action Step: _____

5. _____

Today's Action Step: _____

Step 3: Write your "To Do" list. (Locate your frog!)

1. _____

2. _____

3. _____

4. _____

5. _____

6. _____

7. _____

8. _____

Evening Follow-Up

Step 1: What are three things I did well today?

1. _____

2. _____

3. _____

Step 2: What could I have done better?

_____

_____

Step 3: Read your "Affirmations List"

Thoughts from the Day

DAY 21

IF YOU HELP ENOUGH OTHER PEOPLE...

"You can get everything you want in life if you just help enough other people get the things that they want in life."

– Zig Ziglar

One of the great paradoxes in life is that the best way to help yourself is to help others. There is something magical that happens when you lose yourself in the service of others.

Many times when I am counseling someone who is depressed or frustrated with life, the best advice I can offer is for them is to forget their problems and go help somebody else. Service can cure all wounds. Quite often, serving others is the last thing we want to think about. We want everyone else to serve us because we are in a bad mood or having a bad day. We want the attention. As human beings we are naturally a little bit selfish. It takes a conscious effort for us to think outside of ourselves.

Why is it that so many wealthy, famous and powerful people end up taking depression medications or resorting to addictive and destructive habits? It is because so many of them have spent a lifetime looking for ways to get other people to serve them. They have focused for years on whatever it would take for them to succeed and be wealthy. Somewhere along the way they forgot to use their increased wealth and opportunity to help other people around them. And in the end, they are left with fame and fortune but no friendship. They can have all of the possessions in the world but have nothing with real value. They have everything they want in life but at the same time, nothing they really need.

Try this experiment some day: go through an entire day trying to help everyone around you. Don't ask for anything from anybody, only what you can do to help them. Here are some examples:

- Call a friend just to talk or see how they're doing.
- Do a chore around the house that normally your spouse has to do.
- Do a job at work that normally a co-worker would do.
- Write a "Thank you" note for someone who wouldn't expect it.
- Ask, "How can I help?" when someone has a tough task or is having a tough day.

There are thousands of ways you can help and serve people around you. Just keep your eyes open for the opportunities. You will find that the more you help them, the happier and more fulfilled you will feel throughout your day. All the money in the world will mean nothing if you haven't helped others along the way.

The Scarcity Complex

Why is it hard for us to share our time and good fortune with other people? It is because most of us operate from a position of scarcity. Deep inside we feel like there is only so much wealth, popularity, and happiness to go around. So if someone else is succeeding, then we can't be as successful. If people are talking about the great accomplishment of someone else, they must be saying that we aren't as good. It is completely crazy and false thinking but it is at the center of a lot of human behavior. It is the reason we feel like we have to criticize others. Our brain says, "There is only so much good to go around. If people think less of them, it must mean that I'm better than them."

We need to always remind ourselves that there is plenty of room at the top. There is an abundance of greatness and happiness out there and enough for everyone to share. We don't become successful by outwitting or beating down everyone else. We can do great things and so can our neighbor. You can be the best and so can the guy you don't really like. Ask yourself if you are truly happy when you hear about someone else's accomplishments. Or are you a little jealous? Do you feel like you have to say, "Yeah but that guy used to do this..."

All of those criticisms and ill-feelings for other people often come from our own position of scarcity. When we are happy with ourselves, we will also be happy with others.

A Challenge

You have just spent three weeks learning and applying the principles that will help you live life more fully. You are already enjoying the benefits of the effort you have put into this program. **Make sure you think about others in your life that could benefit from this process.** In truth, everyone can benefit from working on these principles. They are the same principles that great people have used for centuries. Don't keep them to yourself. Share them with those around you and they will thank you for it.

This book was written with a great desire to help as many people as possible. I believe that we can each be an instrument in bringing happiness to those around us.

When you help others, you are really helping yourself.

DAY 21 WORKSHEET

HELPING OTHERS

"We are all angels with just one wing, and we need each other to fly."

- John Hagee

Challenge: Think about people in your life who could benefit from learning the principles in this book. Share it with them. Your results will be more permanent if you can help other people to achieve the same results. The more you help others, the faster you will reach all of your goals.

Step 1: Read Your Affirmations List

Step 2: Write your Definite Purpose with daily action goals

1. _____

Today's Action Step: _____

2. _____

Today's Action Step: _____

3. _____

Today's Action Step: _____

4. _____

Today's Action Step: _____

5. _____

Today's Action Step: _____

Step 3: Write your "To Do" list of other tasks to get done today

1. _____
2. _____
3. _____
4. _____
5. _____
6. _____
7. _____
8. _____

Evening Follow-Up

Step 1: What are three things I did well today?

1. _____
2. _____
3. _____

Step 2: What could I have done better?

_____

_____

Step 3: Read your "Affirmations List"

Thoughts from the Day

Review of week 3

Week 3 In Review

Congratulations! You have finished all 21 days of the "3-Week Miracle"! Before we move on to the final assessment, let's review what we learned in the final week:

Day 15 – Crossing the Rubicon

Talked about the big decisions and decisive moments in our life where we have to leave behind the security of the past and take the step toward our future.

Day 16 – Defying Gravity

In this section we identified the thoughts, attitudes, people, etc. that were acting as the gravity holding us down.

Day 17 – Criticism

"It is not the critic that counts..." Any time we make a bold move we will face criticism. Often times the critics are those who are jealous of our goals and ambitions.

Day 18 – Larry Bird

In this story we learned about the years of hard work and preparation that go into the ability to perform confidently in one decisive moment.

Day 19 – The Four-Minute Mile

Many of the barriers we place on ourselves are merely psychological barriers that we can break through. Remember, if someone else can do it, there's no reason you can.

Day 20 – Don't Bounce the Pitch

When we set a goal, let's go after it with all of our energy and ability. We don't have time in this life to give a half-effort. If it is worth doing, it is worth doing well.

Day 21 – Helping Others Helps You

The greatest work we can do in life is to help others to be happy and successful. There is no reason for it to be lonely at the top. Bring someone with you. Share what you have learned and feel the joy of helping someone find joy.

Now you can move on to the final assessment where you will be able to measure your growth over the past few weeks.

Thoughts from Week 3

Final Assessment

FINAL ASSESSMENT

So here we are at the end of our 21-day experiment. You should be excited that you have stuck with it this far. I know that if you have worked through this book and written your goals every day, you are feeling and acting a lot more positively and confidently. You probably don't need anyone to tell you or show you how much you have changed but I think it is fun to quantify it.

On the next page is the exact same quiz you took at the start of this book. <u>Don't look back at your previous answers or score</u>. Take the quiz and answer honestly about how you feel today. After taking the quiz, check back to your scores from 3 weeks ago and add them to the "previous" column. Now compare them to your new scores. If you have put the effort into completing this program every day, I guarantee you will see a jump in your overall score. It is impossible to work through this program diligently and not improve your scores.

STATEMENT	ASSESSMENT	SCORE	PREVI-OUS
HOPE			
I believe in my ability to change my life.	Less True 1 2 3 4 5 More True		
I see my financial situation improving in the next 5 years.	Less True 1 2 3 4 5 More True		
I believe that I can be happy.	Less True 1 2 3 4 5 More True		
I feel optimistic about the future.	Less True 1 2 3 4 5 More True		
I face adversity and opposition calmly and with hope.	Less True 1 2 3 4 5 More True		
	Total Section Score =		
	Average Score (Total / 5) =		

PERSONAL MANAGEMENT			
I put time into improving my job skills.	Less True 1 2 3 4 5 More True		
I put time into improving myself.	Less True 1 2 3 4 5 More True		
I know the principles to employ that will make me successful.	Less True 1 2 3 4 5 More True		
I am efficient with my time.	Less True 1 2 3 4 5 More True		
I tend to my responsibilities without being asked.	Less True 1 2 3 4 5 More True		
I am willing to work hard to improve myself.	Less True 1 2 3 4 5 More True		
I focus my thoughts on positive ideas and goals.	Less True 1 2 3 4 5 More True		
I do something to better myself every day.	Less True 1 2 3 4 5 More True		
I gratefully accept advice, correction and criticism.	Less True 1 2 3 4 5 More True		
I work hard, even when I'm not under pressure or close supervision.	Less True 1 2 3 4 5 More True		
I focus my efforts on the most important things.	Less True 1 2 3 4 5 More True		
I keep a balance between work, family, rest and self-improvement.	Less True 1 2 3 4 5 More True		
I am patient with myself as I overcome challenges and obstacles.	Less True 1 2 3 4 5 More True		
I am always punctual.	Less True 1 2 3 4 5 More True		
	Total Section Score		
	Average Score (Total / 14) =		

Personal Worth and Self-Esteem			
I believe in my ability to become successful.	Less True 1 2 3 4 5 More True		
I feel confident in who I am and the choices I make.	Less True 1 2 3 4 5 More True		
I am grateful for that which I have.	Less True 1 2 3 4 5 More True		
I am happy with the amount of money I make.	Less True 1 2 3 4 5 More True		
I enjoy my current job.	Less True 1 2 3 4 5 More True		
I feel I have something positive to offer those around me.	Less True 1 2 3 4 5 More True		
I feel genuinely happy when others around me succeed.	Less True 1 2 3 4 5 More True		
	Total Section Score		
	Average Score (Total / 7) =		

Goals and Vision			
I have a clearly defined vision of where I want to be in 5 years.	Less True 1 2 3 4 5 More True		
I have clearly-written long and short-term goals.	Less True 1 2 3 4 5 More True		
I set daily goals for myself	Less True 1 2 3 4 5 More True		
I review my actions from the day and look for ways to improve them.	Less True 1 2 3 4 5 More True		
	Total Section Score		
	Average Score (Total / 4) =		

Love and Charity			
I show gratitude to the people who help and support me.	Less True 1 2 3 4 5 More True		
I make time to be with my family and loved ones.	Less True 1 2 3 4 5 More True		
I enjoy the benefits of a strong family.	Less True 1 2 3 4 5 More True		
I forgive those who have offended or wronged me.	Less True 1 2 3 4 5 More True		
I treat my family with love and respect all of the time.	Less True 1 2 3 4 5 More True		
I actively look for ways to help other people.	Less True 1 2 3 4 5 More True		
I try to understand the feelings of others and their point of view.	Less True 1 2 3 4 5 More True		
	Total Section Score		
	Average Score (Total / 7) =		

Total Test Score (Not including averages from each section)			
Total / 37 = Average Score			
Improvement	+		

Congratulations! Your score went up! How do I know your score went up? Like I said, it is impossible to honestly do this program for 21 days and not have an increased score!

What does a jump in your score mean? It means you are feeling more confident, more grateful, more focused, and happier than you were last month. You know where you want to take your life and you are confident in being able to achieve it. You've put in the effort and you deserve the credit. You should be proud of yourself for accomplishing what 99% of people around you aren't willing to ever attempt! You are a miracle!

FINAL ASSESSMENT

"That which is measured, improves."

- Karl Pearson

Challenge: Review the results of your self-assessment and compare them with your scores from the first assessment.

Which areas showed the greatest improvement?

1. _____

2. _____

Which individual questions showed the greatest improvement?

1. _____

2. _____

3. _____

4. _____

5. _____

What are your thoughts about your test results?

_____

_____

_____

_____

Conclusion

CONCLUSION

Well, you made it! Three weeks of vision, goal setting, positive thinking and self-assessment. You deserve to be congratulated for sticking with it. You really have done more than 99% of the people in the world to improve your life.

You have learned and put into practice the Laws that have led great men and women to success for centuries. The consistent practice of these principles is more valuable to you than an MBA from a prestigious university. Why? Because they are practical and they are personal. You can apply them to any area of your personal life, any occupation, any relationship. The world is full of "educated" derelicts who spent many years and many thousands of dollars on an education that they can't seem to apply to anything. You have an advantage over them. Education alone has never made anyone successful.

Now that we have finished your "formal" training in the Laws of Success, I hope that you don't look at this as the end of a book, but as the beginning of a better and more successful life. Look at the results you've seen after just three weeks! Imagine an entire year of goal-setting and action plans!

I wrote this book to help as many people as possible. I want you to have a happy and successful life and I hope that I have the opportunity to hear your success story and what you have accomplished by applying these principles. We all have one pass through this life and in many ways our success doesn't come from what we accomplish as much as it comes from what we can help others accomplish. If you know of someone who could use a boost or a kick-start, please let them know about the 3-Week Miracle.

Always remember that the principles of success have been the same for centuries. You have learned them in a few weeks. What you do with them will determine your future. Develop your vision. Write your goals every day. Use the Law of Attraction to bring opportunities into your life. Read your "affirmation list" every day to build self-esteem and program your subconscious for success. Eat the frog. Break your four-minute mile. Ignore the critics. Defy gravity from time to time.

More than anything, remember that you are a miracle. You are more complex and amazing than anything ever built or conceived. When you come to realize it, your life will change. Be who you were meant to be. Be who you have always wanted to be. Don't let the your doubts keep you from sticking your neck out and going after your dreams. You create your own destiny every day.

Kris Heap
krisheap@3weekmiracle.com

RECOMMENDED READING

There many books that I love and that have shaped my life. Here are a few of them that I think you may enjoy:

1. ***As a Man Thinketh*** – James Allen
   The first "self-help" book I ever read. Given to me by my grandfather on the day I graduated high school. It taught me that my internal thoughts affected my external results. Written over 100 years ago and still applicable today.

2. ***The Greatest Salesman in the World*** – Og Mandino
   The second "self-help" book I ever read. This is a wonderful book about how a young merchant becomes the greatest salesman in the world through self-mastery.

3. ***The Alchemist*** – Paulo Coelho
   This allegorical novel about a shepherd boy following his dreams has sold over 65 million copies and been translated into 67 languages. It is a captivating read and subtly teaches the value of holding firm to one's dreams.

4. ***The 4-Hour Work Week*** – Timothy Ferris
   This book fascinated me. It is rich with ideas on how to reduce the stress in your life and how to be bold in creating the lifestyle you want. This one was a game-changer for me.

ABOUT THE AUTHOR

Kris Heap is a dentist from Mesa, AZ. His passion is helping people achieve a more fulfilling life. His lectures teach participants how to take control of their life and achieve more than they thought possible. Kris also spends time as a photographer, a bluegrass musician and, most importantly, a husband and father. He is extremely excited to publish his first book, *The 3-Week Miracle.*